**DO NOT REMOVE
CARDS FROM POCKET**

STOP CALLING ME MR. DARLING!

STOP
CALLING ME
MR. DARLING!

CAROL BURDICK

PAUL S. ERIKSSON, *Publisher*
Middlebury, Vermont

Manufactured in the United States of America

10 9 8 7 6 5 4 3 2 1

Library of Congress Cataloging-in-Publication Data

Burdick, Carol.
    Stop calling me Mr. Darling! / by Carol Burdick.
        p. cm
    Correspondence with Edward Darling
    ISBN 0-8397-7897-X : $15.95
    1. Burdick, Carol—Correspondence. 2. Darling, Edward—Correspondence. 3. Poets, American—20th century—Correspondence. 4. Editors—United States—Correspondence. I. Darling, Edward.
II. Title.
PS3552.U7115Z485 1988
811'.54—dc19
[B]   88-19197
                                                     CIP

To my children and to my students
with love and gratitude for holding me steady
on the tight rope until I discovered my own
sense of balance.

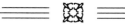

STOP
CALLING ME
MR. DARLING!

791 Lawrence Ave.
East Aurora, N.Y. 14052
November, 19__

Mr. Edward Darling, Editor
Beacon Press
25 Beacon Street
Boston, Massachusetts 02108

Dear Mr. Darling:

Our mutual friend, Don Johnston, suggested I write to you, but I do so with great reluctance, feeling it may be an imposition bordering discourtesy.

Is there any place in Beacon Press publications for poetry? I am in danger of taking myself seriously as a verse-maker and Don isn't helping me steer away from this because he thinks some of what I say "speaks" to the reader. I have had positive reactions from a few others (including Ciardi, Fromm and C. Day-Lewis), but only rejections so far as publication is concerned — except for one little avant-garde journal which accepted me out of curiosity, I think.

The verses rise from a sort of suburban conscience; they deal, generally, with human flaws, failures, hopes, and questionings. (Good Lord. How pompous-sounding *that* is!)

What I would like to do is bundle them all up and send them to someone who has experience in publishing and who is not prejudiced from knowing me, thus wanting me to succeed at what has suddenly become so important.

This is asking, probably, an impossible much, and I shall not become hemlock-minded if you respond negatively.

Unassuredly yours,
Carol Burdick Hudson

November 19, 19__

Dear Mrs. Hudson:

If you stop writing you will be, in my judgment, committing a sin of major proportions.

You manage a deft touch of genuine — no question about it — modesty combined with a fortitude which has never learned defeat; and I'm saying it must never.

My judgment is made on the basis of your prose. The language is your servant; this can be said of few persons.

Now come down off that cloud and let's sit at the table; and as the behemoth of American popular culture, Pogo, would say, Don't splash.

God in heaven knows that most writers of verse — hell, let's say most poets — why cringe? — have tough sledding. I've read several bundles this fall, and some of them seem to me good. But the names are unkown and the authors, while they are willing to be artists, are not willing to be workmen; at least, to judge by their actions. They don't know what media are publishing poetry, or what kind, or at what price; they do not follow Hamlet's directions to the players. All they do is write poetry. And that's not enough.

Beacon has published only two books of poetry: John Holmes and W.T. Stace. We ought not to—it's not fair to the artists because we don't know how to sell poetry. But many university presses, particularly Princeton, do fairly well. Others are U of Pittsburgh, Michigan, California, Wesleyan, Rutgers. Also World and Scribners.

If you'd let me know where you've tried, perhaps I could help. I think trying to publish a whole volume before you publish individual poems elsewhere is pretty optimistic, but I don't really know much.

Maybe you need to talk to an agent. Your library has a copy of *The Literary Market Place* by R.R. Bowker; and in that yearbook there are about six pages listing authors' agents. An agent listed there is trustworthy; and he'll take 10% of whatever you receive as his fee. But it's his business—it's his livelihood—to know who wants what among publishers. If I knew an agent who specialized in poetry, I'd tell you the name, but I don't. One of them would probably know, and you could pick one that sounds promising from the list and simply inquire.

After you've got a little reputation from having published—anywhere—a small handful of poems, *then* you have a background for suggesting a small sheaf in one volume. Maybe you've already come to that point—you give a hint in that direction. I'm wondering about those magazines that turned you down: did you really write for their markets or just submit a poem? How about your local newspaper? Your church bulletin? A one-act play for the church school? *Anything anywhere . . .*

For a while my sister-in-law made a substantial amount of money a year selling poetry to the *Christian Science Monitor* alone; then they suddenly dropped her for reasons I don't understand. I cite the instance merely to indicate that it can be done.

Do you follow the information in *The Writer* at all? I happen to know Abe Burack rather well, and I know that his magazine has helped some people by listing markets and suggesting who wants what.

Did you ever stop to think that the Greeting Card people pay out a whale of a lot of dough yearly for quite *bad* verse? I mean 50 cents a line and up.

Well, I'm rambling. I'd like to help, especially since Don says he likes your work; but you've picked, of course, the toughest part of the writing world to enter and you have to be indomitable.

I should really ask you to send me some samples; but even if I liked them very much, I have no idea how to market them except to plug along according to the lines I've already named to you. Would any of the poets you mentioned be willing to sponsor you at all? One of them might say to another editor, "I'm asking Carol Hudson to send you a couple of things and I've told her you'd give her stuff some consideration." No more than that — it would be darn helpful.

Yes — I know: you shrivel at the idea of pushing yourself. But that's part of being a workman, damn it. If you don't, who will?

I think you should be writing all kinds of stuff—not just poetry. But this is a jungle in which every beast must fight talon and claw for his own survival in his own way; the only method I really know is the one which reminds us that you die if you stop trying. Artistically, I mean.

Look—if my word would be of any use to you, go ahead and send me 20 verses and I'll tell you honestly what one man thinks. More than that I cannot do anyhow. Just don't give up.

Cordially,
Edward Darling

cc: Don Johnston

(Note: Perhaps only an aspiring writer can quite understand what this first letter from Edward Darling did for and to me. Years later I can still feel that impact: not only had he taken me seriously, he had spent his time to advise and encourage. I put the "bundle" of verses together and sent them off with a note saying they were delayed only because our house had caught on fire. Then I waited . . . and waited . . . and despaired.)

By the Kitchen Window

With coffee and a cigarette
I sit a moment, pondering
which is more intense —
the daily life
of mother-wife
or the separate one of words.

Spring sun falls soft
across drab lands;
it warms my hands.

Birds outside this glass
are free to fly — to sing.
But in my heart
is set apart
a silent place, untouched by sun,
where self is struggling
with itself
to find an answer.

Is the battle won
if I renounce
this word-love need —
or should I heed
my writer-self?

The sunlight fades,
a child calls my mother-name,
and I return (lest supper burn!)

to surface living and my housewife face,
still not quite able to erase
the question.

Up From The Grave He Arose!

Rejoice all ye of little faith
whose minds reject
our fundamental origins . . .
Rejoice that Easter Day has passed
without disaster,
although our memories
tugged and pulled,
carrying us back to churches in the vale
where the children that we were
listened to the preacher say
Christ had risen on this day
to save the world. Of course,
we were the world.

  Somewhere along the way
we lost that sense of saving grace
and gained a nothingness — with just a trace
of bitter lack, a hunger for a truth
  that's true no longer.
So let us pray! (for lives less hollow, scarred);
  with Easter gone it may not be so hard.

Incorrect Superlative

I'd always thought
   the Cat
was cruelest of animals.

The Cat
   will catch a mouse
   he doesn't need to satisfy his hunger,
   and slowly disembowel it, —
   watching, clinical and calm,
   as his victim shakes with pain and fear;
   allowing it to run
   on an invisible string
   before flexing his most superior muscles
   to capture it again.

The Cat
   enjoys listening
   to the squeakings of the mouse.

I'd always thought
   the Cat
was cruelest of animals.
But the Cat

   Kills, at last;
   strolls, ego-satisfied, away —
   to seek another mouse, perhaps . . .

The Cat
   is not
   the cruelest of animals.

February, 19___

Dear Carol: (Hudson)

Your little sheaf of verse arrived just as I began to get into a Christmas rush of outside engagements and so forth, and things seem to have been pretty breathless ever since. Now I have a chance to come up for air, and I want to speak to you.

I am assuming that the Lawrence address is still correct and that you were able to reconstruct the place — what an experience *that* must have been . . . My God, it makes one's blood run cold.

But to work, men. There'll be no strike today.

COVER LETTER. I like it. No suggestions for change.

BY THE KITCHEN WINDOW. This is partly poetry and partly prose. The situation itself is real enough; but I'm not sure how many people want to see a woman struggling with herself over whether to be an artist or a mother; and there is always the question whether the presence of a doubt does not answer the query. I keep thinking of Harriet Beecher Stowe, who wrote *Uncle Tom's Cabin* with a wooden stirring spoon in one hand and a quill in the other while the kids pulled the cat's tail under the table . . . Can anything but death stop an artist? In any event, my taste does not run to works which explain how difficult the craft is or which are too damned self-conscious about the fact that one is a sh----! writer; and since this is in your mind in the following two verses, I extend my comment at this point. It is your privilege, madam, to invite me to continue my downward path into hell, as it is mine to express a personal viewpoint. Shall we dance?

MYOPIA. I earnestly dislike "And then I sit and write a bit . . ."

FORGET IT. Same objection about discussing the craft. *Do* it and stop weeping or talking about it.

SNARL. It's a version of HOWL; it's a legitimate emotion. I'd leave it as it is.

UP FROM THE GRAVE. Could you make the first lines refer in general to enlightened minds rather than specifically to Unitarians? I think that would improve it.

ADRIFT BETWEEN KIPLING AND CORSO. Objection sustained: the poet-mother again. This is too status-conscious. A writer is only a writer, for God's sake!

OF SOMEONE I KNOW. Your rhyme-requirement hurts this. Driftwood doesn't come from the ocean's core. Why are the sands bloody? I get the idea, all right but it needs cleaning. It's mixed. The Sculptor who wounded you in the carving picked you casually, by chance? I'll admit you've got something here worth working over, but what? God exults when he has cleaned you off to the bare spirit? In which case, why worry about the next wave?

INCORRECT SUPERLATIVE. Best so far. I think "he doesn't need to satisfy his hunger" should be two lines, the first ending with "need." And I never saw a cat disembowel a mouse, but maybe so. The poem is good.

MOTTO. Who can argue with this?

(How I hate the woe which fills me —
I'll be cheerful — if it kills me!)

FRIDAY. No — I think this is prose, pure and simple.

COMPLAINT. Many great poets, as you know, have argued about what is the proper *subject* for poetry. Frost could have done this; you had trouble with it. I call this prose.

SMALL SERMON. I think this is true insight, and a very good figure, too.

TRIAL BY WATER. Good. I'm for the dock, myself.

NIGHT QUESTION. Swell.

POSEUR. Good, good, Nice balance.

AS TWIG. Two different subjects. Your boys had a good day which horrified the writer. I think that's enough. The try at philosophy which follows satisfied neither writer nor reader — actually you gave up yourself.

ON GETTING FAT. Isn't this unfinished? And what do you mean by the most important word in the poem, "restlessness"?

INSTRUCTIONS FOR A DAUGHTER. Acute. Yes, yes.

THE CENTRIFUGE. I don't think this makes it. You've failed to pick the single point you're trying to sharpen. What has contemplation got to do with death-wish?

AND BUILD ACCORDINGLY. I'm glad Ciardi liked it. To me, poetry is not the proper tool for an argument with a critic. If Alex Pope wants to, he's got the whole 18th century for company.

AMATEUR. This gets awfully prosy; it's choppy; there is neither the dignity of powerful metrical emphasis nor of lyric feeling. Maybe that's just right for a mathematician. But not for love.

SMOKE LAKE. Now I call *this* terrific. Real feeling, good observation, carefully thought out and well said.

DESTINATION UNKNOWN. There's a wry thing here that I like. Maybe you have more of this in you — mordant sarcasm, satirical mockery.

MY FATHER CHOPPING WOOD. How do you *know* he is hoping for death? This could be done in the first person — your father speaking — and done with authority.

FEARFUL DISCOVERY. "Have lived without it —" without what, soul or reason? I think you can do this one better. The idea that you abandoned God but he did not abandon you — you're right, it's the Francis Thompson touch, the Hound of Heaven — is powerful potentially; I'll bet, personally, that if you did this poem in pentameter, unrhymed, it'd come out better unless you want to try a lyrical imitation of Francis . . . I think your rhymes sometimes lead you away or force you into corners.

Well, Carol! I've read them all and I found some I liked, as you see. You really shouldn't care what I think. Poetry is fiercely personal. Yet Frost and Robinson and sometimes Kipling and even Rupert Brooke and of course Housman — some of the lads — and Millay and Emily and some of the girls — managed to get the fiercely personal across; and so do you, quite often. I said before, you mustn't stop. Now please discontinue being self-conscious. You are godawfully selfconscious. You say to yourself, "Egad, I'm writing a poem. Look ma, no hands!" Cut it out, and get back to your paper.

Cheerfully,
Ed Darling

(Note: I fell down with rapture but arose with despair, my most available emotion during those emerging years.)

On Getting Fat

Restlessness returning,
burning within,
requires feeding
of some kind.
Yet
there is no food or drink
for such hungering;
nor can
manipulation of the mind
decrease the yearning.
Appeasing this
with oral panaceas
society condones
(pastry, liquor, cigarettes),
only lets
the body add to flabby flesh
covering
its starving bones.

Instructions for a Daughter

Put the red queen
    on the black king, child —
the red goes on the black;
once you've put the card down, dear,
    there is no turning back.

Deuces are not wild, sweet,
    cheating isn't fair —
but when you lose
    you can start again;
(that's in solitaire, my dear,
    just
        in
            solitaire . . .)

Smoke Lake

set
in autumn's late bronze hills,
fills
— incredibly sapphire —
the eye;
until
blue glides at night
toward topaz;
horizon pales to gilded curve
above
the jutting blacknesses.
Light
fades,
fails;
leaves, when color's spent,
blue-stained retina
and visceral content.

February 9, 19___

Sir:

Ten watts worth of Woody Herman on the stereo; "Lost in Space" and quarreling kids in the t.v. room; husband chatting with a young foreign guest above the music; a sixth grade test on Spain and France getting moldier in my briefcase; the cat promising instantaneous kittens; hair that needs washing *now;* the telephone punctuating the confusion — and all I *want* to do is get this g.d. letter written before I sink into meringue-like amiability — or something.

To hell with Harriet — Harriet is irrelevant.

Like Lin Yutang, I am divided — not only between tears and laughter but also between an embarrassing amount of gratitude and a flaming desire to argue with you, using untipped foils.

Since I was raised to believe that people only like "nice girls" I'll probably choke back caustic commentary and expose only the ladylike reactions.

No I can't

Yes I will

Ambivalence reigns.

It is a great relief to have the two-faced fantasy finally punctured; the morbid one sure you had found total nothing in form and content; the manic envisioning your *insisting* Beacon publish a small volume right away, preferably one with gilt-edged pages.

Right now, after reading, re-reading and re-re-reading your comments, there is no particular depression — no measurable elation. You left me out on my miserable limb, but didn't, at least, chop it off.

If this candor comes through as a lack of appreciation for your time, energy and good-nature, I really am failing to communicate. (Any thank-you sounds feeble-minded to my "godawfully self-conscious" ears, anyway!)

I still would like to send you occasional bits and pieces. If on casual "My God — not another one!" reading, you see anything you strongly like or dislike, you could indicate by a + or − sign and return in the self-addressed stamped envelope. At least you would be a kind of yard-stick.

Do I try to sell any of these? Scratch that. I *shall* start sending out the ones you liked — and maybe some you didn't. Has anyone ever accused you of being anti-fe-male?*

Split-levelishly,
Carol Hudson

*Rhetorical question, only

(Note: Only a real amateur could have dared to so demonstrate all the less lovable qualities of a leech. Along with this prickly letter, I sent a new verse called "Gestation," marked "throw away." Sure that I had now succeeded in alienating Mr. Darling forever, I moped — and haunted the mailbox.)

February 23, 19__

Dear Carol:

First of all, I won't throw out "Gestation" because I like it. I think you've put something very hard to describe into words and found for airy nothing a local habitation and a name. That's Shakespeare, kid, not Edward.

Why do you sheathe your claws in my presence? Aha — I know: you think I'm an Editor. I am Sir Oracle and when I ope my mouth let no dog bark. That's Shake-speare, too.

Any old time you feel like sending me a verse, send it, in the name of freedom of the press!

You know what I think makes poetry? It's the evoked beauty of the living picture, as in

"Part of a moon was falling down the west/Dragging the whole sky with it to the hills . . ."

But God forbid that I should pronounce my "theory of aesthetics" to you; the experts have done it before. I doubt if I'm a very good critic, especially of modern free-wheeling verse which so often knows no discipline and so often takes the easy way. Your "Gestation" is full of suggestions, though, and it contains also one very poignant living picture properly evoked. It speaks pages.

Don't be *grateful,* except in passing. Not overweeningly. Not to *me!*

You know who's publishing a good deal of verse today and doing it beautifully? University of Massachusetts Press, Munson Hall, Amherst, Massachusetts, 01003. I've had several review books from them lately. Why not try them?

The severest critic you should listen to is Carol Burdick Hudson. *She* should give you hell all the time — and I think she does. She should also tell you sometimes, "You've *done* it, daughter."

Cordially,
Ed

(Note: By now I was helplessly, hopelessly in thrall . . .)

February 28, 19___

Dear Mr. Darling:

Although I vowed not to be a nuisance, I've been holding such an impassioned colloquy with you for the past two hours (while wielding a dishrag and a broom), I have finally decided to bring the words into being and see how they look. (They may appear rasher than I deem prudent.)

First, in order of unimportance, I am pleased you were responsive to "Gestation." Surprised, too. However, I can only go on sending you things if you do *not* feel obligated to put your response on paper.

Secondly, — how in hell do I approach the University of Massachusetts Press? Head-on? A reticent query? Name-drop? Obliquely? I've been both daunted and dented by a terse rejection from the *C.S. Monitor* this week. I am a good teacher, a questionable writer and a very poor peddler. The verses come with relative ease (because they are addressed to me, I suppose!) but writing letters to unknown individuals is "orful." (The only way I could ever have been bold enough to communicate with you, for instance, was because Don said you would not bite. If this sounds coy, too bad.)

Thirdly, — you did not quite level with me about Beacon. A friend put *The Sound of Silence* in my hands last week and if those are meditations for Lent, I'm a saint. They are highly personal verse-inquiries into being. I doubt if an audience — even with the "Meditation" from *Thais* as background — would find them particularly profitable for contemplation and higher things-type thinking. Furthermore, I'm not at all sure that my verses are not more honest — and nearly as skillful. I know my stuff speaks to some people very closely.

Before you aim this toward the nearest wastebasket, let me try to summarize. If Carol Hudson's verses are simply not good enough for BP or UUA to trifle with, Carol Hudson should be told in just those words. Quote: "Your verses, Mrs. Hudson, perhaps show a laudable attempt to express your obvious, rather incoherent feelings *but* they are not good enough to be published." Period — 30 — Unquote.

This is the turning-off, the icy shower that I need. (I'm too much of a romantic coward to do it to myself.) Then, hopefully, I could return the feelings to cold-storage and start being fulltime mother-wife-teacher again, living on a busy and useful surface level.

I thought I had made this clear before, but perhaps not. Don is concerned for my soul, I'm afraid — and perhaps for my sanity — but you can't be.

This is not an unsheathing of claws, Sir Oracle — this is a sodden and probably rather silly attempt to reveal a forlorn, rabbity ego. Or is it id?

Well, I'll get off the couch now and go fold some laundry.

Uncertainly,
C. Hudson

March 31, 19__

Dear Carol:

How do you approach U of Mass? Good God! You write to

The Editor
University of Massachusetts Press
Munson Hall
Amherst, Massachusetts 01003

and you say:

Dear Sir:

I have noticed your production of several books of poetry lately which I thought were very beautifully presented; it makes me yearn to have you look at some verses of my own with a view to possible publication, and I have the temerity to send you 20 samples under separate cover, to give you an idea of what I am trying to do. If you would like to see more, I can only tell you that I do have them ready to send. If what I am producing is not of interest, then I have intruded only briefly. Your courtesy will be much appreciated.

Sincerely,

Pretty tough, huh?

Don't be daunted or dented by rejections. I once plastered a room with rejection slips.

I remember *The Gate of Silence. (Note: He had this title confused with another book to which I had referred — it all gets cleared up a few letters further on.)*

It sold about 45 copies and the author is a famous philosopher, too. I don't see quite where I didn't level with you — I *told* you we'd published Stace and added that we don't know how to sell poetry. What's unlevel about that? Every house has its special character. Beacon does not publish fiction, drama or poetry. We steer clear of them. It's sort of a House policy.

You're dead wrong to say I'm not concerned with your soul or with your sanity. I don't know what the first *is* but you've got plenty of the second.

Christ, if you'd written the number of pages I have that ended in the fireplace you'd change from tears to laughter and remember that if it didn't work the first time there is only one answer — only one: try again. I just burned to ashes 30 one-act plays and 150 pages of another book that stinks. So life is tough? Art is hard to accomplish? What do you know . . . !

Best,
Ed

(Note: Shortly thereafter, I sent some more verses — he refers to these in the next letter — along with a note saying that my lack of ability to cope with my current existence was frightening enough to make me wonder about consulting a psychiatrist. What I did not say — and what I was not saying to anyone, including myself, was that my twenty-year marriage was foundering — and I thought I might be going down with the ship.)

April 28, 19__

DOC.   Not so sick, my lord,
As she is troubled with thick-coming fancies
That keep her from her rest.
MACB.   Cure her of that:
Canst thou not minister to a mind diseased,
Pluck from the memory a rooted sorrow,
Raze out the written troubles of the brain
And with some sweet oblivious antidote
Cleanse the stuffed bosom of that perilous stuff
Which feeds upon the heart?
DOC.   Therein the patient
Must minister to himself.

Carol my dear:

I have never seen your face; I have no idea what your age is; all I know of your experiences is that you have loved, borne children, and had your house burn up: and suffered that excruciating irritation (stimulus, if you prefer) of the cranium that makes expression necessary ("For well, dear brother, I know/ That if thou didst not sing, thou wouldst surely die . . .").

Not long ago your verse was so goddam personal that it was self-conscious. Shall I be a wife and mother or shall I go into a garret and be a poet? At that point I was very rough with you and told you that you had to be both. I still believe it. And I think that's the way it's working out. The bland soul, untroubled, has nothing to write about. The pearl is a disease of the oyster.

But what's more, you have a saving sense of humor — to which you give a short shrift and a long rope, as they used to say in the old outlaw days. Yep — you don't give your laughter, your risibility, your perspective, your sense of the ridiculous, half as much exercise as you do your sense of savagery and tumult and tragedy. They're both yours, Carol. One need not exclude the other. Which is a part of discovering Carol Burdick Hudson.

Psychiatrist's couch, bah. Throw physic to the dogs! Your own insight is increasing as your ability with words is growing. These later pieces are much better than what I first saw. Part of your trouble was that you weren't *sharing*. That's why you felt the necessity of publication. Being human, you must share. It's no good if you don't — no good at all. One cannot be a poet alone by oneself. The audience is as important as the writing. And now you're beginning to share and to get reactions. Terrific! I see hope. A sail, a sail! And you're right about the diary. Writing *is* therapeutic. I assert it as a divinely-revealed truth. There is simply no doubt of it.

Listen: I would print — and I *will* print, under certain circumstances — EVE ASKS FOR EQUAL TIME: SELF-PITY: ALONE: and I would print PLEA, I think, except for the godawful line "in saline-blurred precision," for which there is no excuse. Saline-blurred, for Christ's sake! *You don't talk that way and you don't think that way.* Even "through tears that blur precision" would be better than *that.*

SELF CONFIDENCE is almost good: but you require "extrovert" to carry more weight than it is capable of. Not even an extrovert could pat a porcupine and not get hurt unless the needles were down flat. Something's wrong here; but the idea is worth looking at.

ATTEMPT gets wound up on its own rhyme-scheme until the figure gets mixed up in nonsense. *What* could circle on its arc? Only answer, grammatically, is "moment". Or is it "commotion"? One makes sense, and the other doesn't, and you're not clear, and it becomes an exercise. You see I am talking to you in unbuckled candor. And I may be wrong as all hell. But an artist never admits that except in private to another artist. Never to the customers — that's what I mean.

THIS CAN'T BE AGONY is that old self-conscious, "Look, I'm a poet — I suffer as I work with verbal symbols." You mustn't say it: you must *show* it.

I said awhile back that I'd print . . . under certain circumstances. It was you who put the idea into my head:

THE SOUND OF SILENCE was an assignment which Ray Baughan accepted from me: to compile a book of "meditations" or "aspirations" or "thoughts" for *Lenten Manual*. I had no idea he'd write poetry. When that's the way it turned out, you should have seen the correspondence: we were working them over like madmen as I kept insisting he could have anything he wanted but merely asked whether so and so would be better than so and so — to which he graciously agreed, most of the time; but often he rewrote a poem entirely, or chucked it for a different one. It was lovely agony. But I would have printed anything he insisted on, because once he accepted the assignment it was his book, not mine.

With you, if we go ahead, it will be your book, not mine; but it won't be a book until we've agreed on a final version and in this case I'm the boss because I'll be trying to publish a short book of verse to sell for a small sum in the *Lenten Manual* format (paper cover, stapled not sewn and only about 40-50 pages in length). It will probably lose money, so I can't offer any advance; but if it does sell 2000 copies, you should then get 10% of the list price on every copy sold thereafter. Roughly, that's what I have in mind as an experiment. And if I can make it with you, then maybe I can do others, too. And if we break even, Beacon might be willing to take it over for hard cover.

Roughly, that's what I have in mind. Three of your poems are already acceptable as they stand, as I've already said. Want to try for six? Want to try for a dozen? If you get to 40, we'll go to press, and on my head be it. I think it's a worthy experiment; I think you've got something to say that will be enjoyable and helpful to other people. And we can go at it in our own time in our own way and print when we're ready, without pressures of deadline. You wanna try?

Cheerfully,
Ed

P.S.   Stop calling me Mister Darling!

(Note: Almost too stunned to respond, I seized the nearest piece of writing material at hand — a postcard with a picture of a dappled fawn on it — and after scrawling a large "YES!" on the message side, ran all the way to the post office.)

A soberer Tuesday
May 4, 19__

Dear Mr. Darling:

One of the nicer parts about writing to you is that it gets a little easier each time — although right now I'm regretting the silly postcard — it was the only bit of mailable material available at that precise moment and I plead "not guilty" to any symbolism regarding the misty-eyed fawn. I hope it did not frighten any secretaries along the way . . .

Brother, have you handed me a gift-wrapped goal! I have moved through my teaching hours since in a kind of gentle daze through which the voices and bodies of the children are seen as remotely as pond-weed viewed while floating on one's face in the water — abstractions of movement rather unimportant to the viewer.

With "adequate precision"? No, I'll look for some word to convey wrenched but condensed emotion. (Not look — feel for.) I also think the third stanza might be dropped completely.

Should you be warned there are a few of the lot which I will fight to have included as they stand? Of course by "fight" I merely mean maneuver, manipulate — not mandate.

Auden says: "In the desert of the heart
                    Let the healing fountain start"
and this booklet of yours-mine could be *the healing fountain* — although perhaps that's too sedimental.

When a tape is made of the local Readers Workshop program, "Poetry of Carol Hudson" I am going to ask that you listen to it. Much of my stuff is more intensely aural than eyeable. People *do* react to it — and do not tire of it quickly. I am aware that the listenability may have something to do with the fact that in my relative uneducatedness, the only words I have are ones which I use in speaking. This tends to put me somewhere between the intellectual and the fancier of Edgar Guest, so far as audience is concerned. The people who do react are, in many cases, people who do not ordinarily read poetry. Two thousand copies sounds like a billion.

Since you have made this decision to limb-balance, would you re-read the few from the first batch you saw and see if any of them stand? (other than the mother-wife variety you are always unbuckling at me about). I am thinking of SMOKE LAKE, INCORRECT SUPERLATIVE, and a few others.

No, Mr. Darling, you do not know my face — but you've certainly taken a comprehensive glance at a part of my "soul" which has been under lock-and-key for some time. I hope you see it correctly, because you seem to have more confidence than I about its ultimate self-acceptance.

I'm sorry if you object to being called Mr. Darling because I will not use a first name with anyone who means so much — and if that sounds really kooky, tough. I am.

Of course the Macbeth dialogue is about me (and 1,000,000 others). (Except, perhaps, the "stuf-fed bosom" which rather leads one off.) I can see I will have to brush up on my Shakespeare — a sophomoric six credits were sadly wasted on the giddy youngster of so long ago.

How are you on the Bible? I've been thinking about the devil's leading Jesus to the mountaintop and displaying the world—but there goes that messianic complex again.

If you are ever *ever* sorry about committing yourself even this much, please tell me. So long as I go on not believing, it will hardly hurt at all—and the sheer bother may get to you.

Queries: Would it interest you to know which verses local U-U ministers have used with sermons? May I still send out verses to sundry magazines? Will you let me correspond with you from Africa if my husband's Peace Corps application is accepted?

One last meditation for the day. I am not especially honest; I nurse many unresolvable conflicts with masochistic care—but I am not too tender to accept criticism and I will try to deal with you as truthfully as possible. If I do not agree with your reactions you will damned will know about it.

It may not be so much a dance, you know, as a duel—but in your own elegant phrase—

I wanna try!
Carol Hudson

May 10, 19__

Dear Carol:

Well, then it looks something like this: we have ready (or almost ready, pending slight amendments) about 18 poems. *(Titles followed.)*

You should now make up a sheaf of these in what publishers call "fair copies" with a carbon: you keep the carbon and prepare the originals for me. Don't mail them. I want everything at once.

Let's go on from here. Fifteen or twenty more and we're pretty close to a booklet, pretty close to publication. Let's not promise it — let's have a look when you're up to 35 poems.

And be thinking of a title for the book. I like *Destination Unknown* pretty well as a starter . . .

Destination Unknown
And Other Poems
By
Carol Burdick Hudson

Hm?
Ed

(Note: Whatever response I made to this — and there must have been one, along with another bundle of verses for him to look at — is lost. Usually I wrote the first drafts of my letters to this still unbelievable figure in my journal and then typed an improved, shined-up, yearned-over revision to send off to Boston.)

Destination Unknown

run woman run!
> *(run from yourself*
>> *run from your thoughts*
>>> *hide from them!)*

no.
> *I am tired of running.*
> *I will bury myself under words*
>> *like piles of dead leaves . . .*

oh look!
> *look woman look!*
> *they are being blown away*
>> *by the dry wind of reason*
> *and there you are*
> *indecently exposed to yourself.*

run woman run!

June 3, 19__

Dear Carol:

Now that we are working together, I have taken your stuff to Cape Cod where I can work without hearing a phone ring or being asked to attend some goddam meeting. All I hear there is the songs of the birds and the roar of the distant surf (if the wind is NW) and the breeze in the pines. I'm not going to try to edit your material in this office!

You may find periods of silence, but it will be friendly silence.

There are no laws: send me what you want to send. Send me what you believe in.

I intend to answer questions; and if I don't you must repeat them. For example, I think *Destination Unknown* is just great. Let us by all means work with that title.

> More later—
> Ed

June 25, 19__

(Note: Attenuated past endurance by not hearing as soon as I innocently, impatiently thought that I should, I mailed the following postcard):

Check where appropriate and return to sender:

_____ Yes, I received the second batch of verses
_____ No, I did not receive the second batch of verses
_____ Yes, you should send the rest
_____ No, you should not send the rest

> *Friendly*
> *Silence*

(Note: In returning this card, Mr. Darling had scribbled on it: "Send anything you have confidence in. There is only one *book ahead of you now, so I should get to yours soon. Hell, I gotta write a letter." Ed.)*

June 28, 19___

Dear Carol:

As you see, I found the postcard inadequate.

Lissen, I certainly *should* have acknowledged your second batch, and I could swear that I had done so, saying that I would try to take the material to Cape Cod where I can read in peace and not be interrupted by the telephone all the time. You got no such letter?

Anyhow, the situation is this: I am editing another book of verse which I commissioned 18 months ago. It's next year's *Lenten Manual,* and I'm about half-way through. Until I can finish this, deadlines do not permit me to get wound up in anything else. I'm hoping—as I have hoped every day since the manuscript of the *Lenten Manual* arrived—that I could finish it "this" week. Well—!

You're next. Keep the faith. The chin: up, but not out. The spirit: calm, reflective, independent as a hog on ice. The mouth: quick to smile in recognition of our human condition, which seems to require us to take ourselves—and I mean me—too damned seriously.

Send anything whenever you want. Ah'm yo' fr'en, Chile.

Best,
Ed

June 29, 19___

Sire:

> I have an irksome itch to write —
> Not poetry, not prose, not dialogue —
> But something to communicate
> With partially existent "friend"
> Who will accept the tepid burbelings
> As built-in disadvantage of his job;
> Will quickly scan this vapid scrawl
> Then toss it, crumpled, in the trash —
> But hold no rancor for his minutes lost
> Toward perpetrator of unasked-for lines.
> (More perfect audience could not be found —
> No fury, no refusal — and no sound.)
> or something . . .

Yes, I received your wind-from-the-NW letter but did not understand it was the second batch you were referring to. Now I know exactly what is happening. Thank you very much. (Can I help it if I keep thinking you have changed your mind — or found it again — and the whole shootin'-match has been called off?) It's *not* that I am in a hurry — after all, what is time to anyone as old as I am? All I will do is gently remind you, "Sir, I exist!" (hoping you do not reply as Crane's universe did to *his* challenge . . .)

A young friend has remarked that "destination unknown" sounds like an old John Wayne movie. Let's *not*. I'd even prefer *The Unwilling Seed* or *Paltry Poetics* or *Nauseating Novelties* or just plain *CRUD*.

The only trouble with you is—

Correction—

The only trouble I *know* about you is: twice you have said "Send any poems you have confidence in." It is not the ending preposition which strikes perturbation to my very depths—it's the beginning assumption.

I do not have confidence in *any* of them, goddamit. Lack of confidence is my only raison d'etre. If I were overflowing with confidence I wouldn't be the same person, I wouldn't need to be saying those verses. In fact, I shun the company of people who *are* confident. *Confidence is a ten letter dirty word.*

No, I am not drunk—but it's an excellent suggestion. Thank you.

> Hurriedly (and with
> receding chin)
> Carol B. Hudson the first

(Note: This self-pitying bleat was sent along with the comment that I was beginning to think of him as a red-headed leprechaun. But he had dealt with crushes on the part of aspiring authors before, I suspect . . . viz. the final paragraph in his next letter.)

July 5, 19___

Dear Carol:

It can be said, I believe, of almost *anyone* that "putting it down on paper" is therapeutic; but of nobody more than of you; and perhaps the reason is that you have a visceral drive to produce on paper which runs the mating instinct a very close second: I'm inclined to think so. You just *want* to see your brainchildren in print, and you want it with such a passion that I am inclined to say, "This must be." I believe it must. I think you're dauntless and will not give up, in short.

"However," replied the Universe . . .

But I am not the Universe; I *have* a sense of obligation!

Destination Unknown does not sound like anything but *Destination Unknown,* and whatever we adumbrate comes from a complex of personal impressions. However, I don't insist on that title. *The Unwilling Seed* is very good as a *title.* Does it have any meaning?

Stop being so cautious: the only trouble with me is that I am Edward. What is the only trouble with You? Right, the first time.

Final prepositions should have stopped being a pain to you long ago when you broke the bonds of custom, convention, and the expectations of the best thought-of people.

If you had confidence in them they wouldn't have to be written! What utter rot. Whitman knew better: "For well, dear brother, I know/ That if thou didst not sing, thou wouldst surely die." Honest appraisal of one's effort that finally concludes with a judgment that it is, while far from perfect, at least a respectable effort, is no 10-letter word. Did I send you a copy of *Old Quotes at Home?* I have confidence in it for a very small audience which includes at least the author and his artist, and maybe a few others . . .

I am, madam, a rather stout five-foot-eleven with grey hair and four grandchildren. It would be better for me to read than hear, since I must judge on the basis of reading. Write when you feel like it!

Cordially,
Ed

". . . because it's there"

Despair can be a height and not a falling:
  the dizzy precipice, the nightmare peak,
where isolate, a climber clings
  with bloody fingertips, eyes shut against
the rushing air which rings with echoes
          calling..............calling
          (reminders of remainders):
Despair can be a height and not a falling.

Despair can be the place for hanging on
  or even upward crawling with hardly breath;
letting go in easy plummet to the space below

would be a simpler ending; Death
or madness less appalling
   than clinging to crumbling cliff
where desolate are echoes
               calling..............calling
               (remainders of reminders):
Despair can be a height and not a falling.

Robert Graves Said

Robert Graves said
"poets must be lovers . . ."
Yes, they must.
But some never get further
than loving themselves;
these are the frigid,
narcissistic
who — trying to hold
a mirror to the world —
can only find reflected
their own putrid images.

July 14, 19___

Dear Carol:

I'm going to be typing this myself, so bear with me.

First thing you ought to do if you're really interested in using the extrovert ditty again is to look to see if the *Journal* is copyright material throughout (it surely is) and then write to the editor for a letter giving you permission to use it again elsewhere. She cannot refuse. You save the letter giving permission. And in the future when you submit, you might make it a condition of the contribution that you are offering "first rights only," which would save you the trouble of getting any further permissions.

Now let's see — where were we?

I've just had a nice cool luncheon, and believe it or not, I'm going to start on old Carol.

I have now separated a voluminous correspondence from the poetry. It was impossible to tell you what was here and what was duplicated and what was missing.

In my letter to you of May 10, I listed 18 verses which I told you are acceptable for publication. I have another score or so which need decisions, here in this office; and a group at the Cape. Let's work on those that are here — would that be reasonable? Or shall we go to the Cape?

ATTEMPT. I'm returning this one herewith. You're not sure of it yourself, and you're so involved with the technical details that the motivation for writing the poem has become an attempt to resolve a mechanical problem. There's cleverness in this as an exercise; but I feel no powerful emotion driving you. I say the thing's an exercise. If you want to disprove it, then write the poem you intended.

SELF CONFIDENCE (this must be your "extrovert ditty"). I wish you'd start with a real name instead of "my friend." The poem begins as if it were a vocative, as did FDR, "My friends—"! The name Elizabeth would fill in here just right; but you pick your own. "That's just her line" fits in very well, but I'm not sure how much *meaning* there is in it. *What* is just her line? Being superconfident? Or patting porcupines? Or do you mean, "That's just a line of bull from her"—? I can't be sure. *Otherwise,* I like this poem, and let's call it No. 19.

THIS CAN'T BE AGONY. I think this is dreadful, but maybe it's just the thing for *Evergreen Review* or some of those rough-and-tumble outlets. The visual imagery is pretty confused: you are spouting blood because the words tear you, but your soul is hanging impaled on them. Hold that metaphor! And who says true agony is mute? I'll return this one.

(Note: The preceding comment is as embarrassing to the writer today as it was when it first came across the desk. Talk about a bucketful of cold water . . . ! Anyway, it served to abort any number of self-pitying, deep-purple verses.)

BECAUSE IT'S THERE. You say despair can be a height and not a falling: but your picture is of a person *about* to fall, or in danger of falling—and the terror is of falling. Therefore despair remains a falling, dammit. Despite this, I like the lyric quality and the use of the refrain. Really this is quite a clever piece. But I do not think you can use "isolate" to mean "isolated." The Elizabethan age ended in 1616 when Willie died. If you'd say "Where—all—alone—

a climber clings" that might do it; but "climber clings" is an unhappy alliteration. Can't you get the idea in here that he is looking *up*, struggling up, not willing to fall? Because the end of the verse heads that way. I really think you've got a poem here, if you'll back off and reconsider it. Let me enclose it for revision, hm? But don't give this one up.

GESTATION. You marked this "throw away," but I would not throw it out. The trouble is that we don't see the conflict: those first two lines suggest it, but not powerfully enough. I think it's up to you to explain what the conflict really is: and think twice, because this is important. How can you emerge from elemental slime unless you're *in* it? Okay, then you are stating that you *are* in it. Yet you mean it as a figure of speech — the elemental slime of smug satisfaction with mediocrity, or some damn thing . . . This against what you *will do, will be,* will achieve . . . want to work on this? All you're asking for is understanding, a hand to hold when you're in trouble. I tell you this is worth some pains. But I'll enclose it for your editing.

WONDER. Job actually defied God to do his worst; his cry was defiance to the end, not an admission of insignificance. Am I wrong? But that doesn't matter. I think WONDER is the wrong title; but I think the poem is honest and fresh and technically very interesting. Let's call it No. 20, and meanwhile if you want to revise it at all, you go ahead. It's a good idea though, and you've handled it skillfully.

ROBERT GRAVES SAID. When he said "poets must be lovers" did he not mean "able to give love"? Thus he would have — and did, in my opinion — rule out the narcissistic from the beginning . . . And why "putrid"images? Decomposed, rotten, decaying? Even so, you have an idea. Maybe you could make it satirical: He thought he was a great lover; boasted that he was; but his only real love was himself: something along that line? I'll return this one and you think it over.

Well now — that's all the time I have for that right now, but you should be somewhat mollified, now that we've got *started*. Trouble is, I leave for Europe a week from today . . . Oh, well, — only for three weeks!

Look, I'm being awfully frank with you, because that's the only way to be thoroughly honest; so for heaven's sake, don't wonder what else I mean between the lines, because I've *said* what I mean out loud — not to discourage you but to pique you, to motivate you, to make you do your best. Nothing else. No hidden meanings; no mental reservations!

Best,
Ed

(Note: More than "piqued," — for I was still laboring under the amateurish assumption that strong feeling creates art — I felt punctured. I dashed off the following letter, and had reason to regret my impulsiveness later on.)

July 16, 19___

Dear Pruner:

This vine is a bit shaken by your recent letter—
perhaps I will understand my own reactions better if I
verbalize them. I honestly don't think that it is the criticism
of the verses—or the suggestions, or whatever euphemism
one employs, which has staggered me. It's the rather over-
powering realization that I've failed so in communicating.
Now wait—don't click your tongue at me or shake your
head or whatever editors do at times like this. F'rinstance—
ATTEMPT was written two or three days after discovering a
close friend, an irreplaceable person in my life, had a brain
tumor. I had been weeping and feeling that how-can-he-
bear-this, how-can-I-bear-it hopelessness until the time at
Woodspring when in three hours I wrote the first copies of
PLEA and ATTEMPT. I know the sonnet form drove me
down hackneyed paths but it was no "exercise," it was a
terrible craving to lengthen Bill's time. Perhaps it was only
selfish catharsis—but it worked—it let me deal with my
emotions and with these friends and even be strong enough
to stay with his wife the night he died, being helpful instead
of sodden. I know it isn't a good poem. I never really
though of publishing it and shouldn't have sent it to you, of
course. Perhaps someday I'll revise, keeping the phrases I
still like. But it's difficult to accept the fact that *none* of the
emotion was transmitted—and there will be other blows,
too, as we go along, I suppose, equally severe.

I think there will be times when I will not like you very
much. Is that allowed? Will you mind my telling you?

The pattern emerging looks a little like this:
Verses from CBH to ED
        Reaction from ED to CBH
    CBH gets all defensive & argues each point
        CBH settles down to revision
    CBH sends verses back to ED
Is that the methodology? I hate to get all "functionally fixated" (that's a gorgeous term I picked up last week at a creativity conference which, along with "Bloom's Theory of Cognitive Domains" furnished me with lots of jumping-off phrases for scurrilous doggerel) — but I've lost track of my syntax, a warning that I should give up and go to bed. The sunset is gone, the mosquitoes are convening around the Coleman lantern, the rest of the family is tucked into the tent. We are on our way to the Maine Coast, camping tonight at a Finger Lakes State Park.

Europe? Wow!

Witheredly (not for long),
Carol

P.S. I'll retitle JOB, but I think it follows "J.B.", at least fairly consistently.

(Note: Out-of-sight was certainly not out-of-mind. I continued to bombard Mr. Darling with letters, even when I hadn't any revisions or new work to show him.)

Self-Confidence

"My friend,"
*   our daughter said*
*   (in some distress),*
"thinks she can do most anything —
I bet she'd even try
*   to pat a porcupine!"*

"That's just her line,"
*   was my reply,*
"Oh yes,
*   I know the type —*
an extrovert. . . ."

(but with their *luck*
*   it might not even hurt!)*

August 9, 19__

Preamble: Are you aware that some of my best writing (but worst penmanship) goes into these "missages"?

So welcome home! I promised myself not to effuse in your direction for a long while but time's relative and it sure seems like a long while . . . However, I'll journal along and not mail this for another week or so.

This is our first night at Smoke Lake and the loons are celebrating our arrival while six children (one guest for each of ours; believe it or not, it is easier that way) and my husband sleep. The stars are too close for comfort in this patch of Canadian wilderness, so I have turned my back on the big window. "Peace, like recent rain, pervades the quiet night . . ." That's an awfully nice line if I did say so myself!

Since last "speaking" with you, we have upheavaled our lives completely. Camping in Maine, we met people who knew of a job opening and one thing led to another until now Bob starts a new counseling position in Portland on August 29 and I have landed a 5th and 6th grade language arts position in the same system. We've leased our East Aurora house for a year and will move, as renters, into a little old home in South Freeport on Sept. 5. It is an impractical move, financially speaking, and it is hard to leave our close friends and associates but we want to depressurize ourselves, escape suburbia, if possible. There is mountain skiing two hours away, the hahbah (harbor to a western New Yorker) is a spectacular playground. My husband has Viking genes, I think, and we've decided it's foolish to stall inland until a nebulous retirement. Ah dunno' if it'll work out — it's dangerous to force a dream into reality — but we're going to try it, anyway.

The preceding explanation should be excuse enough for you to be tolerant of my not having done anything in polishing the 30-odd verses you've not seen — and the title is still unclear. It has been sorely frustrating not to have one moment for meditation but it couldn't be helped.

Cliches sprout from cliches when I'm tired — sorry. I'm older, too — lamented a birthday just yesterday.

Come to think on't, you may be relieved CBH isn't breathing down the back of your neck for a while . . .

We spent a remarkable day and night with the Johnstons on top of their Vermont mountain. The only new verse of the summer is theirs. Cynical as I am, it is hard not to believe those two haven't found some of the real answers.

They are comforting just to be near—and I'm fairly sure the comfort comes from the emanation of a rare combination of lovingness and humor.

We also met a high priest of the U-U church while visiting some other friends at their Maine lodge. His wife had some sparkle but he's talked so long he doesn't even listen to himself any more—far less to others. And he's probably a very good minister and I am being catty. I'm not really a Unitarian, anyway—I fall down on the progress-of-mankind creed. Mankind stinks.

Only the loons and I have the Answer. And tomorrow night, if the old brown owl who lives in the deep dark forest doesn't frighten the little peppermint girl into a brittle mess, you'll have the rest of the story . .

> Two or three days and
> many guests later, by
> the potbellied stove
> on a crisp evening

This was our first full day with only six people instead of 14—I hate to give up on it by going to bed. It's been a Carrie Jacobs Bondish end of a day.

About Maine again:

> There's no danger in dreaming—
> but harm may ensue
> from allowing a dangerous dream to come true!

Consider *Eve Asks for Equal Time* as a title? Or from the Job poem, *The Fragile Ultimate?*

I've been reading Sylvia Plath's poetry today and it surely makes me humble. I would, in fact, be depressed by her ability if I didn't happen at the moment to be feeling physically so well. She hurt awful. I've been there some but am unwilling to nourish my pain, even if that means I will never be a good writer. She really bled to death, using words as weapons to inflict self-wounds and as poultices for the gashes. And she wrote the language of poetry infinitely better than I — perhaps because of a more intellectual training, perhaps because she had more perception, more experience — I dunno.

Even though I share her feeling that life is basically black and frightening and futile, I still laugh a lot — and I don't believe she could ever stop hurting long enough to know what sheer idiotic silliness could feel like. She dropped the middle-class morality mask — that safe hiding place — too. So "who is Sylvia?" I do not know, nor what she is-was, either. But I *am* getting to know who Carol is, if not what to do about her.

Except at the moment. Go to bed, Carol!
O.K. —

1:30 A.M.
August 20, 19___

Is it my fault that I start to wake up at about 11 P.M.? Is it so startling that after a day overfilled with cooking, child-watching, sailing, teen-age listening, that these fire-crackling, star-studded, all-by-myself hours are the prized ones of the day?

Of course it's not my fault. Had a maiden aunt with real insight who once remarked: "One thing I've noticed about you, Carol, is that you're never wrong."

I started to rationalize even before I started to verbalize.

This letter is only being written for one of several reasons. You may choose the least offensive:

a. I won a solitaire game; always a let-down

b. The New Yorkers arrived and there are many better pomes and maybe some not-so-better than the versey ones I write which leads me into pushmipullyu thoughts

c. Rhymes have been rampaging riotously round the reverberating rhythms of retreating raindrops; disgusting, facile, trivial rhymes. I am fleeing from the temptation to put them on paper.

> But seriously, dear sir, I am alarmed —
> The "stuffed bosom" has been cleansed of pain
> (which was the motive force as you know well),
> and in the spacious chambers of the heart
> lurks sudden stillness. Now I must face
> a new and awesome question; this:
> Can I compose from a serenity?
> There has to be some tension to create,
> and artificial tension won't suffice —
> My driving gear has shifted out of high —
> (And fuel is made from fire — never ice)!

Thank you Robert Frost, Shakespeare, and everybody else.

See, things like this are happening:

> Closely around me the starry night presses
> Gently revealing a natural way
> To soften the memory of bruises and stresses,
> Quietly healing the feverish day.
> Slowly a peacefulness filters through being
> (sore from the scraping of sandpaper strife),
> Carrying truthfulness, clear to the seeing:
> No more than nature can justify life!

oh urk, urk, urk.

Did you dig that pattern? John Greenleaf might be pleased with my progress. I guess that when one is raised on a diet of "Rock of Ages, cleft for me," and "Christopher Robin goes hippety, hoppety," there is no hop. I mean hope.

Coming home from Maine in the middle of the night (and the middle of the Massachusetts Turnpike) I sang hymns for two hours without repeating myself. How can one find redemption from that kind of saturated brain?

Maybe if I went to some school for writers next summer? Or am I still too "tender" to take tête-a-tête critical tactics? This is hopeless. I'll enclose a couple of others for your:

quick perusal/brisk refusal/sick amusal . . .

Gawd bless us everyone,
Carol Dickens

P.S. I have not yet begun to write. J. Paul Hudson

Sept. 8, 19__

Dear Carol:

It is after Labor Day and therefore you must be ensconced in the Freeport house. You won't be miserable in Maine as long as you get that sort of kick out of taking your dog for a walk.

(Note: This reference is lost, also. We had a golden retriever who later showed up in a Reader's Digest *profile and who did, in fact, take us for walks.)*

The things that save you are, in the long run, at least two in number: your rather exquisite appreciation of nature, and your sense of humor. Also you have sharp personal insights. All three of these are the subject of poetry, whether you are engaged in prosody or prose.

I have been in very choppy waters since mid-August and am likely to remain there for a couple of weeks more; but have faith. Trust in God, as old Ashley Montagu says: *She* will help you.

This is just to answer your news note and assure you that I'm still with you.

Best,
Ed

Sept. 20, 19__

Dear Carol:

A feeling of confusion overwhelms me. I don't know exactly where we stand on what. Sometimes I have made a criticism and you have said you would or would not accept it; sometimes you have rewritten; I have several versions of some things and appear to have lost other pieces . . . Well, it's confusion. But you have letters from me definitely accepting certain ones. So I think what we should do now is for me to scratch the stuff I have here and start fresh with original copies intended for the printer — not ditto copies or carbons — put in *exactly* the shape that you want. I'll go over these as they arrive, and if I have any further criticism or comment, I'll let you have it. You should keep one carbon of these new originals, and they should be numbered or titled in some way so that both of us can refer to them in correspondence. This would be the clean way to do it, to avoid misunderstandings. All "working" copies should either be thrown away or filed by you; and only one "final" copy kept by me in a current file and carboned by you in a current file. Probably this does mean extra work for you; but it's the final lap as we prepare to approach the printer, and I should think you'd be willing to undertake it. I proceed on the assumption that you are.

Now I'll do a little homework, too, just to show you that I don't mind a bit of extra work myself.

This relates to your letter dated August 9, in which you welcome me home. Actually, I've just *got home* . . . Yep, I've heard the loons; and I love your line "Peace, like recent rain, pervades the quiet night." That is marvelous hexameter, with a lovely caesura in the middle — it's almost Anglosaxon, except that the spirit is that of the romantic poets. I just hope that the rest of the poem lives up to this: I'd like to see it in continued hexameter . . . but you moderns, of course, will pay no attention to such a hope. You're all done with disciplines of that sort.

And I'm happy that the old Viking spirit persists; you'll like Freeport. You'll like Maine. At times you may feel fairly primitive, maybe, but what says Levy-Bruhl? *"Dans tout esprit humain, quel qu'en soit développement, subsiste un fond indéracinable de mentalité primitive."* Quite.

Your characterization of the minister from New York is about as sharp as anything Mencken ever said. Beautiful!

You're wrong of course about the loons and you being the only ones who have the answers. I asked the question long ago and got my answer from a grey gull — now both he and I must be added to your theodicy, your pantheon. Mankind stinks for sure; but that's not the *answer*. Because mankind does not always stink in all directions and under all conditions. In short, mankind partially stinks and partially has in itself the conditions of a really quite wonderful salvation, regardless of that old primitive of Levy-Bruhl's.

It's funny: sometimes you are so lyrical that one wonders if you and perhaps Eddie Guest (or in a different mood, Robert W. Service and before that, Kipling and Swinburne — what a stable!) had been having an evening of song together; and other times rhyme and rhythm are anathema to you. "There's no danger in dreaming" is so bright it's almost musical comedy.

You just be *you*. Not Sylvia Plath. Don't be a tragic figure! She had no comedy in her at all.

Best,
Ed

(Note: It finally happened. Although my next letter is lost, it is clear that I must have complained about his not remembering that he had already read the whole poem around the line I quoted ("peace, like recent rain . . .") and to which he responded so warmly in the letter above. Mr. Darling's sorely-tried patience was pushed too far . . .)

Sept. 23, 19__

Dear Carol:

For some people I am a good editor; and for other people I simply am not. Now there is no sense in getting personally and emotionally upset about a simple fact like this; so I accept the fact as one of those inter-personal unknowns which has to be lived with. And I do my best to extricate myself from any editorial relationship that turns out to be contributory to continuing unhappiness. Life is too short and so forth. Tastes differ: consistency is not always mine — I have been caught approving of a poem in June and wanting it rewritten (quite forgetting its previous approval) in September. In other words, you are dealing with a very fallible human. All this is an answer to your letter of July 16 where I get the idea that you found so many things that must be characterized as less than salubrious in my criticism of your material that you wanted to argue for the defense.

I'm not sure whether we can work together or not. This is not meant as a negative criticism of either you or me; I guess it's only natural that you would want to defend what you've written. I guess I do, too. So what we come down to is the author's basic and inalienable right to be himself. If you cannot accept my criticism, and if you do not wish to rewrite a thing after hearing from me, then we are faced with two possibilities: I can change my mind, after further study, and decide you've done it right after all; or I can decline to publish. In the same way, you can decline to rewrite, or you can make a try at rewriting.

If the immediate punch that set you going does not come across to me, that could be because your verse fails. This is what we both risk.

I have a guilty conscience about you, because I feel that I've given you a strong indication that we can publish a small volume, and yet I'm all mixed up about what's to be in that volume. Which is why I asked you to put things in order by sending me a fair copy of every poem on which you have now made up your mind; and I'll decide on that basis.

For instance: I told you bluntly and very candidly what I thought about a verse called ATTEMPT. I did not *mean* to be cruel. But to be less than honest is a waste of time. Now you tell me there was profound grief behind the verse and that it was a cry from the heart and not an exercise in verse-writing. What am I to say to *that?* No—don't shrug. Tell me what you'd answer if you were trying to be the editor!

Well, if we multiply this by 50 or so, we're not going to have much fun and we'll spend more time arguing than in writing verse.

Let me tell you how I think we can work it out. If you send a verse and I criticize it, then your answer is either a revision—which is your total reply to the criticism—or a refusal to rewrite, which leaves the final decision ready to be made, one way or the other. I don't think the detailed argument as to why or what needs to be studied is any help. You have a right as the author; I have another right as an editor; and we both have the right to call the whole thing off with amicable expressions of mutual regret. Does this make me sound like a bastard? I suppose it does. But this desk is high-piled with unfinished business . . . I'm ready to continue if you are.

Sincerely,
Ed

(Note: When the world steadied under my feet, I wrote back. I am no longer sure whether I chose the back of a sixth-grade "creative writing" work sheet on purpose or accidentally.)

Sept. 25, 19___

I've lost my place in dual script, it seems:
   not knowing how I so offended you
it's difficult to choose apology.
   "Encroachment" is the sin, perhaps,
for which I'm truly sorry,
   and promise to put back the proper mask —
be business-like and brief and bright —
(because I cannot bear to see
   the Promised Land become mirage
   as outcome of my own stupidity).
May I, then, send you, dutifully transcribed,
   all the fair copies I can cheat on time to do?
I swear I'll never speak again — except on cue.

Carol Hudson

Oh hell! What I'm trying to say in blanker-than-usual verse
is that "Yes, I would like to continue" — if you still have any
faith in my verses.

   You have been so terrifically good for me all year I can
hardly digest the fact of your present feelings!

C.

Sept. 27, 19___

My dear Carol:

On the reverse side of the sheet on which you replied there is a ditto message asking the recipient to list as many impossibilities as he can think of.

Only one happens to occur to me at the moment: that you and I should quit.

That is an impossibility, given our two temperaments. We *must* continue. *I* want to see you come through; and *you* want to come through. Hence it is impossible that we should throw up our hands.

I do have faith in you and in your expression; and if I have been good for you, that's all I need to know. You may fire when ready, Gridley.

I will criticize with a free hand and an honest tongue; you will react; and we will then decide: each poem on its own. When we are through there will be a book.

Cordially,
Ed

(Note: The following letter refers to one of my August journal "verses": I had not intended any of those scrawls for inclusion in the book. Gradually, I learned to leave such effusions where they belonged . . .)

October 4, 19___

Dear Carol:

You said you were enclosing "a couple of recent endeavors" but I found only the two notebook sheets.

I am a sucker for lyrical verse but highly critical if it is at all contrived; there are some people like Swinburne and Kipling who can make internal rhymes and sestinas and everything—and they seem okay; the lines fall right. Others have a painful time with reverse order and false rhyme. It appears to be a matter of taste, like taste in music, which it is all but impossible to "justify." Enough theory!

The one about the starry night has blemishes; but it would pass in many circles, and it's better than anything that Eddie Guest ever did. The phrase "a natural way" bothers me, as does the frankly didactic nature of your final line; but your line, "sore from the scraping of sandpaper strife" is fresh, alive, new, personal and carries a touch of genius. I object to being "taught a lesson," but sometimes it can be done with such expert grace one accepts it. "When duty whispers low, 'Thou must,'/ The youth replies, 'I can.' " If I'd been the first reader I'm afraid that classic verse would never have seen the light . . .

Of your titles, I like best, best, best: *A Face of My Own.*
Ah — that's perfect. Perfect for *you* and perfect for your
book. I think so.

Cordially,
Ed

*(Note: On October 3rd, I sent Mr. Darling a list of titles in fair
copy format — 31 in all. He accepted all but two, but made com-
ments on all of them.)*

October 24, 19__

Dear Carol:

Thanks for being so patient — at least in appearance —
while you were waiting for the Great White Father to come
out of his omphaloskepsis and make a report.

I return to you herewith the list of 30 verses, anno-
tated.

To put it summarily, you've got 30 poems for the
book; but there are some which might possibly be im-
proved and I'm sure their *order* can be improved. As you see
by my note on Number 14, I now feel that your title should
be *Eve Asks for Equal Time,* and that your title poem should
be the first in the book. I see no reason to omit RETRO-
SPECT — but I am inclined to make it the last verse. Other-
wise you end on a very sombre note — IN MARCH.

As you see, I have questions about 3, 5, 7, 8, *(something* troubles me about 8, but I'm not sure the crack about prose in verse form will stand the test of superior criticism. I may be wrong there, and in any event, I don't see how to improve it. So I'd let it go as it stands), 14, 22, 25, and that's it. Hence I'm returning those pages to you and holding the rest. You should now decide whether you wish to consider what I've said in each case or whether you think it's the way you want it; and then let me have these sheets and any revisions back again so that I'll have a whole set.

Next, I would suggest at least ten more poems, and perhaps 20 more. What do you think? How about material you must have on hand that will increase the variety — a little more humorous verse, maybe; additional stuff about children and the life of the young; about human understanding; about basic satisfactions of life despite the rough edges . . . ? What you've got is good: publishable.

> I await your response!
> Ed

(Note: It seemed to me he was rather more cheerful than the number of "suggestions and comments" warranted — but I had learned my lesson; I held my tongue and put my pen to work. Sometimes the verses were tightened and improved; sometimes they refused to budge. Without realizing it, I was growing into more of a craftsman, able to look at flaws with objectivity, with less panicky defensiveness.)

Retrospect

My Useful Lists
*   were always labeled*
"Do."

Perhaps you younger wives
*   and mothers*
won't
understand my saying
there should have been
a few
*   (more necessary) —*
neatly labeled
"Don't."

October 27, 19___

Dear Carol:

We're in business if our letters are crossing. It's a sure sign. Thanks for the card.

I am sending you separately a book written by another Unitarian. My reasons are several. First, she reminds me of you; second, I want to know how you feel about her work; third, the jacket gives you a contact with the series of contemporary poets.

And fourth, she condenses down to the essence. See p. 64 (which is like you); and study page 60 — which is as delicate a thing as I ever saw from the pen of a cultured and sensitive lady. And tell me what you make of page 20 . . .

I have written a brief comment about this book for our Book Review page; I did it in nine lines because space is short. But I would *rather* run a review by another poet — by you, for instance — if you could do the job in 10 lines or so. I will not be handing my review in for at least a month; and if yours comes to me within that time, I will give your review priority over mine if yours is "any good." Want to try? I won't show you my review because I don't want to influence you.

Best,
Ed

(Note: Not only did I not want to branch out into book reviewing, but as soon as I saw the book, I disliked it — and was horrified that it had reminded him of me. Finally being exposed to contemporary poetry at a workshop run by a University of Maine poet/teacher, I was painfully learning to understand that I was writing in a genre about 30 years "behind the times." So I tried to beg off . . .)

Cinderella hour
Nov. 4, 19__

Dear Omphaloskeptic:

This may turn out to be an off-key, too-too Joycean collection of syllabic sequiturs — nope, I am just too sleepy and depressed to push the pen any further — maybe tomorrow will bring a lightening of my sibelius mood . . .

11 P.M. next day

Do you have the book nearby? Good — prop it up by you and listen.

Here is a statistical resume of my reactions: strongly negative — 38 verses; passable — 22; positive — 20.

The list of titles under the "positive" heading includes #64 without reservation and #60 with some sorrow about the use of "womb" and an uneasy feeling that the desire to "recreate" his image might be a ladylike way of saying something a hell of a lot more earthy (and real). I am not against delicacy per se, so long as the writer realizes what he/she is being dainty about — but I'm not sure this woman is not self-deluded.

So I'm sorry I can't do a review for you — it would not be favorable — even though there are some neat images and isolated examples of a striking phrase. My God how she needed a hard-hearted editor! There are glaring examples of triteness, archaicisms(?) — even syntactical defects, which drown the successful "essencey" bits. Of course, it is apparent that she is hard-working and an intelligent, sensitive person, but surely stock responses like "incandescent dreams," "vision touched the sky," "trust so often spurned," "radiant unity," "bosom of the night," et cetera are in contemporary poor taste.

Mr. D., I hope she reminded you of me because of those 20 or so verses — and not because of the sonnets or the faith-hope-joy-truth ones. I may very well be a worse poet, but my sins are, I *hope,* less purple. Please continue to prune my poems — and let's not let one really trite, standard, overworked phrase get by — unless it is a cliche´ used on purpose in a dialogue.

Lewisohn ripped my KADDISH apart last Tuesday, briefly characterizing it as "sentimental, trite and didactic." He is not God, by the way — what has really happened is that I'm finally reading the good modern writers carefully and my stuff looks just awful to me. Perhaps I *am* a three-name Lady Poet fit only for mothers' clubs and Kiwanis dinners. With the awful facility I have for rhyming, I could make money with greeting card verse and get to be a member of the local poetry society and everything. But I'druther not.

Am I some kind of snob, setting my sights (see? — there I go — trapped in my storehouse of overused language again!) higher than this good lady?

My silly verses I don't feel badly about — having fun with words is permitted, I think. But all the lines which purport to deal seriously with lifesize experience must be looked at with suspicion. Have I found the exact word? Have I conceded sense to sensibility? (You've said these things to me from the very first, but I was too illiterate to internalize the advice — I thought my own, my very own precious emotion *justified* a poem. I am beginning to see and to understand — and perhaps will stop writing anything but the lightest of verse.)

Please I do want the booklet printed but could we profit by that publisher's misdemeanor and keep it *sparse* rather than dropsical?

Perhaps I am merely being morbid, but I don't think so. You see, I have no belief in ultimate virtues — hope, goodness, truth, love. I do not believe truth, for instance, exists — and even honesty is on a sliding scale. Mistress of self-deception since first the ego formed, I will continue to cushion the tragedy of existence with every available deceit — but if I am going to try to write, the words must be as correct, as fresh and as communicative as they can be — within my semi-literate limitations.

All this must be why I reacted so negatively to the book. It is bottom-heavy with timeworn usages, antiquated language that makes me squirm. Furthermore, I think she still does not see herself clearly but as she wishes she were. "A peaceful dialogue" — ! Poetry is not born from peace.

Unhappily,
Carol

P.S. Now I suppose you'll tell me the lady's your sister . . .

Nov. 16, 19__

Dear Carol:

I really don't think I want to let you off the hook on that book review. If you can find 20 poems in a sheaf of 80 that you strongly favor, then you're way ahead. How many books of poetry do you ever pick up in which you turn down more than 20 pages, or mark more than 20 poems? I think *ten* memorable verses out of a hundred would be "not bad." You are involved here with the very great mystery of a mind attempting first to satisfy psychological requirements for itself; and then attempting to reach out for the purpose of communication with other minds. If it succeeds in this latter attempt *at all,* it's a miracle. And if this woman repeats that miracle 20 times, I think she's done a fine job.

The attitude which I have attempted to portray above, my dear poet, is the one with which I attend to your own verse: the experiences Carol has cannot all be communicable to me. If some are strongly communicated, and if I share the emotional experience, I pronounce it a wonderful poem; but I have to admit that a poem which I do *not* share is perhaps (a) very competently done in terms of workmanship; (b) probably very meaningful to the primary audience (the author); and (c) shows a lively mind at work in something better than cliches and commonplaces. In short, whether I "get" it and am touched or not, I see an artist at work and I honor her for being herself.

This is not being said angrily; I'm not cross at all. Not one bit. I just think you owe this poet a brief comment that may help her; and I think you can easily do such a job. My own review occupied nine lines. It identified the author as a Unitarian, and quoted her purpose "to learn what *I* am doing between earth . . and sky . . ." That's *your* purpose, too: the search for meaning. This is religious.

Further, I think it would be good for you to accomplish this review; and I have a mind to send you other books of verse for this purpose, by God.

No, I don't know the author at all. I take it she's a biped who speaks English, but that's the extent of my information.

Your review doesn't have to quote a single verse. You can say frankly that much of it does not appeal strongly to you, but that there are a good handful which you regard as memorable; that you can see what her purpose is and consider her work "deeply sincere and the work of a practiced artist." Hell, there are ways out! I just think this is a growth-experience for you that you ought not to pass up, said he, stroking the long white beard until it glistened again.

What now?
Ed

P.S. Meditation while gazing at the navel is omphaloskepsis; but the person doing it is an omphalopsychite. Any hesychastic knows *that!*

(Note: Accepting what Heaven had evidently fore-ordained, I wrote the review and sent if off to him along with an expressive card from the local drugstore's rack: A figure on the cover says only "Y O U . . ."; when one opens it: "A lawyer once told me that anything I said might be held against me." I signed this "Grrrr"—Mr. Darling returned it with "Purrrr . . .")

December 1, 19___

Carol—

Come on, now, admit I was right to make you do it! Your review is *better* than mine, and I prove it thus: my entire comment is enclosed.

Ed

Bernstein's "Kaddish"
(for Lukas Foss)

A voice
> which hurts each listener
> > with too much love
> > and too great pain
> pours out both pain and love
> upon unaltared ultimate;

beseeching
> "hear me, Lord above"
> > until chaotic clashings —
> > inhumane, so human —
> drown its reaching cry:

then
> from panic's pandemonium
> > rises purest sigh
> > fashioned from an instinct hope,
> a lullaby;

and when
> "forgive me," comes the voice again,
> > "do not forget me, Father!
> > I will promise to believe
> > so you may still exist . . ."
> a living rainbow shimmers through
> > atonal mist.

"Amen   Amen"
> at last is heard:
> the listeners are stirred
> to frantic acclamation —

Yet

> *they hurry from the hall*
> *anxious to forget*
> > *how the music touched them —*
> > *what the voice said.*

December 2, 19__

Dear Carol:

I've been out of the office too much and things have gotten ahead of me. Here, however, is a progress report just before you begin to think I've died in the night.

There are 23 OK poems listed here on your schedule; seven being returned for editorial revision or final decision (that's 30 total); plus quite a few duplicate pages being returned for YOUR files, since I'll keep only one copy of each accepted piece.

I have the 23 in your folder and could go to the printer with them any time. Number 14, EVE, I have marked okay, but I have made a suggestion which you may or may not care for. If you don't, then I accept the poem as is. No. 16 I also accept, but I want to be sure also. No. 20, the title? COMPROMISE for "foreboding"?

I also have your Tentatives 1 to 21, but the morning has slipped away and I have to keep a lunch date and then beat it out of town — so they'll have to wait.

Be of good cheer, Carol. What you've done is really good. Don't worry about my cracks about your psychology. I'm just blathering and you don't have to do anything about it.

More soon.
Ed

December 10, 19___

Sir:

Herewith some remarks, revisions and reiterations:

ALONE. Reworked to the point of madness. It's uneven still but I don't mind *too* much.

SMOKE LAKE. I followed your instructions to the letter.

DESTINATION UNKNOWN. Fair, unmarked, beauteous copy.

EVE. *My* feeling about the last line is that it is a truly *sneaky*, peachy-dandy, down-beat ending, revealing her need to protect her needs from Adam. I may be sorry later but could we leave her be for now?

UP FROM THE GRAVE. This has so much that is bad in it, I don't know where to begin and don't care enough about it to begin, even if I discovered where. Let's add it to the discard pile.

SELF-CONFIDENCE. A different kettle of fish. That line *has* succeeded, although I realize if you zero in on it, there is much to be desired. Unless it is a great blot on our escutcheon, I would like to let it go by.

COMPROMISE. (formerly foreboding), I give you my ultimate affirmation. Reworked the way it lies on the paper, though, so I return a new fair copy.

REHEARSAL. Revised and returned in company with some misgivings. It still may not be successful.

MEA CULPA. Finally settled on a final couplet. "Fiddling" is too expected; graceful and grossly are delightful together. *I* think.

AFTER STORM. This one is so painful for me, I cannot look at it objectively. Would you choose from the alternate endings or simply throw it out? If today weren't so foggy, I might enjoy arguing the permissability of impotent desires. But the fog doth make peasants of us all . .

How'm I doing, Br'er Darling? I feel as if my energy for this had evaporated and hope the sag doesn't show too much.

Dimly,
Carol

After Storm

Mute and purely beautiful this night;
Wind-driven snow at rest
in a tranquility of white,
carelessly crystal under light
  from quiet stars.

So might peace come within my breast,
to fall as snowflakes fall
upon raw scars; to mask impurity,
stifle futile inquiry
which seeks in chaos, reason.
Grant me my white season,
  make me cold.

Cool the scorching flame of why
  down to merest glow;
Come Peace! upon my spirit lie
  like freshly fallen snow.

(Note: The next letter refers to the fact tnat I had been asked if the Christmas verse I had written could be used in a Boston paper — I gave my delighted permission and then was chagrined to find it printed in the Letters to the Editor column . . .)

December 29, 19__

Dear Carol:

Never trust a newspaperman, of course. That goes without saying. But no harm is done, and I have not seen it myself. It does no harm. What the hell harm can it do? It's nice to see it printed, I'm sure. *You* hold the rights, not the paper. We can reprint whenever we wish to, without credit.

Many thanks for the charming little book on grammar and usage. The maddening thing about this is that there is no date in it anywhere. However, as a curiosity I do treasure it — it shall have a place on my shelf next to *The Dictionary of Obsolete English,* which is another treasure and entirely out of print.

When the madness is over and January is upon us, perhaps you and I can finish up our project. I have *never* been so frustrated with meetings and interruptions, so help me — and I have a foot-high pile of sins in front of me which I am determined to clean up before I give up the year.

Happy New Year,
Ed

Hancock Pond Lodge
10:30 of a snowy evening
January One, 19__

Sir Edward:

I am all prickly inside with words and need to communicate. This morning, when the family left to ski at Pleasant Mountain, I started to describe our New Year's Eve for you and got involved in a rhyme scheme which just wouldn't resolve neatly. So instead of correcting papers, the untidy result — pour vous — is on the other side of this sheet. I have worked hard on three poems this lusciously solitary vacation and am excited by the results. Will send you copies when copies are done. They show some sophistication in form and more metaphor than ever before — derivative (but let's hope not too obviously) from the reading and thinking that has been frantically going on whenever the daily routine admits some moments.

Our title bothers me some, Mr. D. Here are a few wilder ones — I wish I could find a statement which would draw attention but also convey my feeling of *knowing* I'm not yet making honest-to-god poems. Please give this a piece of your mind sometimes.

Possibilities:

Poetry rises from *Considerations* (me)

A Conflict with Disorder (Wilbur)

Articulations & Approaches (me)

Poetry must be *Judged by the Heart* (Jarrell)

Poetry comes from *A Sense of Lack* (Eberhart)
Excavations Toward Salvation (Eberhart)
Glances (me)
The Mountainous Molehill (me)
Many Masks, Many Moons (me)
(I also thought of *Reachings* — but *Retchings* is too close at hand . . .)

Too ponderous a title will outweigh the booklet, I know — and I will certainly accept your decision on the matter.

Martin Levin, *Phoenix Nest* editor, just let me invite myself to send some verses, so I bundled up 12 of the shorter and sillier ones, patted them on the head, told them to look carefully before they crossed the street, and sent them off — not really hopefully, of course; I am always rather like a Cinderella with swollen feet.

And I sent the three new ones to Chad Walsh at Beloit, unfairly reminding him of our brief chat after his reading in Portland this fall. Here I have no hope at all, honestly (well, *dis*honestly, then.)

I *am* sort of goofy: a humanitarian who doesn't really like people; a hermit who panics when an acorn drops on the roof; a poet just beginning to know what poetry's about.

Oh dear me suz,
good night.
C.

January 4, 19___

Dear Carol:

Here is your list of Tentative-numbers, with those accepted marked with a check and those being returned for one reason or another circled. The thinking about each one is usually written on the returned sheet.

To me your more recent stuff is so far superior to the self-conscious verse you were writing earlier there is no comparison. In those days you took up pen with the intention of writing a poem, and you were constantly on the alert for subjects. Now the process is different: you find yourself required to express your emotional reaction to some experience, and as you do so it becomes poetry. You are condensing, concentrating, focusing . . .

Let's see how you react to all this.

No fair going off into a corner with a grudge: if you don't like what I say, speak up; if you agree that I'm right, do something about it: I'll join you in song, or argue with you, or do a bare-knuckle job if you feel like it; but all the while I am expressing only one person's opinion, and I could be wrong. So if you want to insist on something that seems right to you, fight for it!

Happy New Year,
Ed

January 5, 19___

Dear Carol:

Somewhere in the works here is my reply to your Tentative list of about 23 poems (I filled a bag with un-answered mail and "things to do today" and spent the New Year weekend at Cape Cod polishing them off; but obvi-ously poor Virginia has to transcribe about ten pounds of stuff before you'll actually receive this missive!).

What I think I discovered is that you are maturing so fast that your material from earlier decades is by compari-son juvenile and should be carefully filed in your closet in case you want to look at it, but not sent out unless, upon re-reading, you are struck by its excellence. You tended to write on any old occasion: *Ha! Here's a subject for a poem!* But now that you are attuned, you're not searching in quite the same way, and the poems begin to come to *you.* It's a not-very-subtle difference; and *vive la différence.*

May I say also that I believe it is a mistake for you to show your editor the various steps in the development of a poem — as if you were saying to him, "You read all the versions and make the comparisons and then tell me which one is best." The work of discovering *that* answer is the job of the poet. Just as a photographer should never show you his mistakes, but only the perfect print. He should *burn* the imperfect ones. I ought to know. I was a commercial pho-tographer. You never show the customer your tricks: only the gleaming perfection of the successes.

Your fifth line is "ski-tired," right? It seems to be "shi-tired" but that makes no sense.

(Note: My heart sank. I had intended that verse only to be a greeting and he had taken it as a submission. Also this was the last time in my life I sent a hand-written verse to anyone.)

I want to ask you how you know the "boys slept dreaming girls." It would be legitimate for you to *guess* they are dreaming girls; but I'm damned if I see how you can assert it. The fact that you did guess this tells us something about you, not about them. Same as with your old man dreaming ocean spray. Who says so? This tells us something about you, not about him. Or the dog his rabbit.

I'm not averse to the I, I, I. Everyone who writes, writes about himself primarily. Montaigne said it, but he was neither the first nor the last to observe this truth.

I like your first quatrain. The whole thing is well enough, and yet—it's anti-climactic. You went to bed. How very goddamned exciting. What a last line! You are out to reconstruct a country house after everybody has gone to bed. Why tell us you're still up seeking for words? I think that is too self-conscious. How about the smell of woodfire; shadows in the old house; the feeling of the dog's fur . . . The gentle seduction of the scene . . . which *could* leave you with an insight about human living and time, while all you say is that the year was dead. "All dream and rhyme, the year slid gently into time," is nice going. But as a whole poem, it's not memorable. But it could be.

As to titles, with a book of verses I doubt if it matters too much. I thought we had something long ago. It's up to you.

Best,
Ed

Titles Don't Matter
An Inner Dialogue in One Act

Time: January 7th, afternoon

Setting: Kitchen table. The outside world is snowy, orderly and beautiful, like a Down East calendar picture. The curtain rises on an argument which has obviously been going on for some time . . .

I: But he wouldn't do it deliberately like that, would he?

Me: If we irritated him enough he might.

I: Why can't you remember we're only a tiny facet of his life?

Me: I suppose we encroached again?

I: You and your big fat happy new year mouth!

Me: His courtesy really got stretched past the showing-point, didn't it?

I: Obviously.

Me: Should we write and tell him we're sorry?

I: No! He might feel constrained to waste his time answering.

Me: Do you suppose what seemed to be saying "Down, Girl!" really meant "Scram!"?

I: I don't want to know. Let's finish the fair copies, submit them and lie low for a while.

Me: You mean be diplomatic and cautious and quiet for fear the book might vanish in a puff of editorial smoke?

I: You got it.

Me: Okay—but titles *do* matter. Even on books of verse. My psyche hurts.

I: So what else is new? The aspirin is in the cupboard.

The End

(Note: I am ashamed to say that I lacked courage to send the above. Reading it now, it seems to have potential for evoking at least a chuckle. At any rate, as the days wore on without hearing from Mr. Darling again, I became morbidly convinced the whole project had gone down the drain.)

February 5, 19__

. . . herewith excerpts from today's Family Letter which was not written with you in mind, so is as unselfconscious as I can be.

Two weeks ago last night, after days of anxiety and a final 24 hours of acute physical-mental discomfort, I gave my first poetry reading at a coffeehouse in Portland. It was a small, smoke-filled, noisy room where, amid the blue-jeaned customers, my black dress and fake pearls looked as out of place as a Tennyson poem in an ee cummings collection. Standing on the tiny platform, I shook so hard the lectern vibrated in sympathy. In my terror, I forgot to introduce the reading by telling them what my son had said, trying to cheer me up before I left home: "Well, Mom, look at it this way. If it's a big flop, you can always go back to being normal again."

Instead, I blurted out something about my not being very happy in this position and that I could only hope the half hour went by as quickly for them as I needed to have it pass for me. I did remember, though, to quote Auden's remark about why artists want to share their work: "to see if the order they have made for themselves out of a welter of impressions makes sense for anyone else . . ." — and then I started to read, my tongue a dull dry clapper in my mouth.

EVE ASKS FOR EQUAL TIME was fourth. When they broke into laughter and applause at its ending (a new one, thanks to Mr. Darling), I began to come out of my icy straitjacket and to realize I had an audience. The proverbial pin could have been heard for the next 25 minutes.

Some pathetic, some beguiling young people came up to talk afterwards. One boy, a nervous bundle, strode over and said belligerently: "You use too much alliteration!"

"I know it," I agreed sadly. "It's a terrible handicap."

After this we became friends. "I write some, too," he confided. "Of course you don't have time to listen right now . . ."

"No, not right now but you could send . . ."

"One starts, 'It was an awful pity' " and he was off.

I contend, with myself as prize example, that there was, is and never will be a more ruthless egomaniac than the Unpublished Poet!

Dear Mr. Darling:

So that's what I wrote to my family, and here is what I need to write to you.

If you were angry, you'd surely blast at me.

If you were through trying to form a booklet, you would be kind enough to let me know, I should think.

If you were sick, surely your secretary would drop a line in my direction.

I've been trying to keep a stiff upper lip and all-that-jazz, but I guess my innards won't take much more. I never really believed in the book (people just aren't this lucky) — so if you've decided to call it off, the main hurt will be to my pride. If you have been ignoring the situation because you didn't want to hurt my feelings, let me assure you I am tough enough to take finality. It's hope stretched taut that is too much to bear.

Carol

It would be interesting to know what happened sometime. This feels more like a nightmare than livingness . . .

(Evidently I re-read the above plaint and decided it was too woeful to risk. I must have managed to write somthing funny on a postcard instead.)

Eve Asks for Equal Time
(for Nicholas Biel, whoever he is)

Could you spare me
just a minute, Sir?
I've been waiting patiently
'til Adam — having talked
himself all out, I guess —
would go to sleep.

How he complains!
Sometimes I'm almost sure
the reason you decided
to make me from his rib
was just to give him someone
he could talk at. Oh sure,
there are the other things,
but honestly, he could not
survive without my audience.

He certainly exaggerates
that business of the being dust
and then so quickly, Man,
all unprepared for manliness.
I've listened to the theme
a thousand times
and never once have said,
"What was so great
*   in being dust?"*
though, goodness knows
I have been tempted to . . .

Oh sorry! that's a nasty word
   "temptation".
I try to never use it
but it just pops out
when I'm not careful.

Adam thinks — and has thought
since the very first,
the burden of our guilt
is on my *appetite —*
which simply is not fair.
That old snake — (he really
  was a darling, in a way) —
used words so well,
persuasively, I guess you'd say,
he made me curious;
(and Adam never told me anything —
not anything that mattered;
never did, doesn't now and
never will — unless I raise
an awful fuss!
(and then he says I nag.)

As for the silly apple,
it appears both you and *Adam*
took it seriously. I was only
flirting — such a little bite
need not have brought
so much of fury and displacement
on our lives. If you had only
been a woman, Sir,

(no disrespect intended)
you might have understood
and only laughed. Women find
forgiveness easier,
though mothers take it to extremes,
I will admit.

Anyway, I know you're tired,
having listened for so long
to Adam. I'm not demanding
anything, I hope, but maybe
you could help me solve my problem.
Adam all the time reminds me
how I was just a second thought
when you had thought him over.

Well, all these years I've wondered
about this: if I'm inferior
and know it, perhaps that's better
than feeling so superior
and still mish-mashing destiny
the way he does. Lord, is one
of us more special than the other?
I'm getting awfully tired
of listening to him grumble —
blame you — and me —
and never once his foolish self!

And I will always wish, I guess,
that you had planned
to make me wholly me —
not just extension

of my Adam's life.
Extension never seems enough, — but look!
he's waking up, —
don't mention this to him;
it's clear
he wouldn't understand
and after all, I am *his wife . . .*

Why Adam, —
did you have a nice nap, dear?

February 10, 19___

Dear Mrs. Hudson:

This is just to reassure you: yes, the last material you sent arrived safe and sound. But Mr. Darling has been on a field trip which involved much preparation, and now that he is home again he is dealing with the mountains of work he left behind him — and with all that accumulated while he was away. And *therefore* — you have not heard from him. He sends you his best, and asks you to be patient and understanding!

He thought your postcard was a beauty — as did I.

Cordially,
Virginia Allen
Secretary

Right after the mail
February 11, 19___

Dear Viriginia Allen:

Thank you for your letter. Would-be poets are no less paranoid than real ones and this particular would-be had constructed a morbid castle in the mire, built on doom and turreted with despair.

Waiting is never my problem. Compared with not-knowing, waiting is life-can-be-beautiful. Feeling disinherited because basically one is convinced of one's ultimate worthlessness is a difficult reaction to cope with. With which to cope. I am still shaking.

So thank you.

Manically,
Carol Hudson

P.S. My regards to your employer, too.
P.S. #2 There really *is* a Santa Claus!

February 27, 19__

Dear Carol:

How other people do it, I cannot say; but for my own self, I have to have peace and quiet in order to do thoughtful editing; and peace and quiet are very seldom characteristics of this office — and that's why editorial work generally ends up at home. As for you, I took you to Cape Cod over the weekend, and I trust you enjoyed yourself. As a result, I have tons of things to say to you — and this will take tons off my conscience because I am very conscious of the fact that I have neglected you. Not because I wanted to, but because of conferences and meetings and interruptions . . . There under the pines, however, with a slightly above-zero wind coming in off the Bay and a roaring fire, plus, thank God, an automatic oil furnace, I was able to read your poetry at ease.

First: I return herewith a sheaf with a 3x5 card on it, marking this as originals which should be your hands for whatever disposal you wish to make of them — they should not be here where they can get mixed in with the "accepted" material.

Second: Please refer to your "remarks, revisions, and reiterations" of Dec. 10:

(Note: There follows a complete list of all the verses submitted and resubmitted before, marked either okay or hold or returning for further consideration. I have excerpted a few samples to show the closeness of his attention.)

COMPROMISE. Okay; retained.

REHEARSAL. I am returning; I want you to try this again.

MEA CULPA. Accepted. This is very good.

KADDISH. I'm returning this with an important question. I tend to shrink from an ending that says, "Now the lesson, boys and girls, is this —" You do have a tendency to tell us what the moral is; but I think it's better without.

AFTER STORM. There are one or two things you should decide; and having done so, I invite you to return a fair copy. Watch out, though, for too many titles with the word "after" in them. This one is well-named, however.

SLOW LEARNER. Okay with some hesitation.

APOSTROPHE. No.

At least you gotta admit that when I *do* give time to Carol Hudson, I give you my full attention!

I think we're pretty close to being in business. Let's see how you react to this batch.

Best,
Ed

Mea Culpa?

millions cry
  and millions moan
wearing hunger at the bone;
    I eat chocolate candy bars
    and gaze upon the tidy stars.

millions groan
  and millions cry
pressed flesh to flesh in fetid tie;
    I breathe prophylactic air
    and play a game of solitaire.

the mad earth spins,
  the planet reels,
they scrape the mud for orange peels;
    I sing songs with graceful rhyme, —
    grossly out of tune with time.

February 25, 19__

Dear Mr. Darling:

Did you write the page of discussion concerning Stutzman's publishing aims? It was masterly, whoever was responsible. We have a fascinating friend who is rebuilding her life and who wrote to us recently, plugging S's "liberal redemptive community." I wrote back that I hoped she found it exactly that but that I thought it sounded like a lot of eggheads getting all muddled up in each others' lives. Group therapy is for experts, not amateurs—and maybe not even for experts, for all the lasting good it seems to do many people.

Oh, and I'm the great one to talk, I who have just been prescribed Librium to remove a weight on my chest and a tightening in my throat. Damned doctor can't understand those are words stuck in my craw that need to be released and disciplined and communicated. I will be my own analyst if it kills me. (It's true that I would prefer to have creativity rather than anxiety be the driving urge. I am that coward who dies, daily, a thousand deaths!)

Perhaps my nine-year-old daughter is wiser than her mother. I found this in her notebook yesterday:

A MORAL
Poetry has no law
but with a flaw.
Bother me I won't let it
Let's go out and
just forget it.

!!!

Enclosed is a copy of a letter to A.S. Burack — a letter I will not send until you do give me permission to use your name (it had to get written while vacation gave me a little time to think).

Dear Mr. Burack:

Edward Darling has given me permission to use his name when writing you but he neglected to tell me exactly how to use it, so I'll just drop it in neatly and hopefully: Edward Darling.

He also advised me, some time ago, to get down into the marketplace and fight for a hearing. Since I am agentless, this places all pugilistic responsibility right on my shrinking psyche and I am forced to clench my teeth and clatter across the cobblestones, courageously whispering, "To the fray!"

Would you be interested in printing the enclosed satire on the type of writing so often perpetrated today by the "poet" who thrives on his/her own "I-centered" sorrow? It contains five short "examples" purporting to be different approaches to the same soggy theme. Others who have read this have found it funny.

The title is the first line, of course, of that ancient and satisfactory couplet: "Malt does more than Milton can

To justify God's ways to man."

For Milton, read poets, but if this is too obscure it could be changed.

Thank you for your time. I've probably approached

you with minimum finesse but at least I remain

Scrappily yours,
Carol B. Hudson

(Note: Mr. Darling returned this to me with the emendation that the couplet was from A.E. Housman's Shropshire Lad, *LXII, and with the letter that follows. It holds some excellent advice, which by this time I should not have needed to hear.)*

March 1, 19___

Dear Carol:

I really don't think I'd submit that material to Burack, because I can't see his using it — not in *The Writer,* which is his magazine. Have you studied the magazine? You should, before submitting . . .

Your verse in this piece has color and merit, but you're using it for the wrong purpose. Parody is one thing; didacticism another. Steer clear of the homiletics — you're often tempted to preach; and that's wrong for the modern poet.

One other hint: I would not be so chatty with a strange editor. I know you, and so I understand how the warmth and passion of your outgoing and very verbal nature is served truly in your letter; in fact, I'm ready to say that you can write good humor, which is a real compliment. That courageous cringing "to the fray" is a small masterpiece. But not to Abe.

To him I'd say something like: "The enclosed is submitted for your consideration at your regular rates. Incidentally, I have your name from Ed Darling, whom I believe you know. But please don't hold him responsible for the enclosed." No more — that's businesslike and pleasant, and it's enough.

Nor would I ever send *anything* to an editor in ditto: then he wonders where else you're submitting at the same time, and his first reaction is not to take a chance.

By this time you've had my new handful of notes . . .

Best,
Ed

Rehearsal

A 'miserere nobis'
       sung
by the skillful,
untouched young,
has meaning now
for both heart and ear
of listener
beyond the age of song:
it seems
         all wrong
somehow,
the middle-aged
are not equipped
to sing: skill disappears
and vocal cords are atrophied
        (like dreams)
by all the tone-deaf years.

Hancock Pond
March 4, 19__

Dear Mr. D. —

"How other people do it, I cannot say; but for my own self I have to have peace and quiet in order to do thoughtful" *writing*. This, editing and writing must require in common. I was delighted by the Cape Cod weekend my verses spent with you and hope there may be future visits! (I'm only being ironic, or sardonic, or ambiguous, or what-haveyou because I've scrambled all weekend to try to get enough time to work on your last suggestions and did not succeed in so doing — and that makes me Sad.)

I did accomplish a sorting-out task of sorts and for your editorfication enclose what I can only hope is a list similar to yours of how the material stands as of March 4th; it all gets rather muddlged (unintentional "g" but it heightens the word), however I do have faith and understanding and hope and an overwhelming feeling of gratitude. "IdoIdoIdo" like the Cowardly Lion.

Some filthy child has wrecked the right hand parenthesis on this machine and I'll never be able to write parenthetically again. Oh woe.

Your advice about not sending "Why Malt" to *The Writer* is herewith acknowledged and will be observed. I won't do it. Maybe a market for this (I thought and still think it is Funny) (the parenthesis is working again) will introduce itself.

I cannot send you any current material because there isn't any, except for some chaotic, neurotic spewings which I am entitling Vomit 1, Vomit 2, etc. Thought I had throat cancer before the holiday. You know — death and disfigurement and the noble suicide and all that stuff. The doctor didn't *quite* laugh at me as he assured me many teachers come to him at this time of year with "identical symptoms." The thought of having identical symptoms hurt my pride some but I am swallowing the prescribed tranquillizer with ease. I submit that I am no "sicker in the head" than almost anyone else — just a helluva lot more articulate about it! Please laugh at me — I am. (But continue to take some of my past poetry seriously because that is my fortress.)

Upon the re-reading of the foregoing, here is a capsule summary: I am frightened by the intensity of my sorrow and am forcing it upon you in an attempt to make the burden lighter by the telling. My brother, a hardened veteran of psychoanalysis, didn't make things easier by assuring me recently that a "do-it-yourself" therapy (e.g., the writing) was the most dangerous kind — and I am feeling endangered, I guess.

Now — won't it be a relief to turn to the next page and see a tidy, unemotional List?

Reflectively (and not liking it),
Carol

P.S. A share of this afternoon has been spent going over your comments on all the verses. You will probably never quite understand how stunned I remain at being taken seriously. With all your reassurances, I keep wondering if my stuff doesn't get to feel to you like a nagging, abcessed tooth one knows *has* to be taken care of (and whether you would tell me if it did!)

> A HERO DIES BUT ONCE
> . . . but if practice really perfect makes
> a COWARD has the final breaks!

C.

(Note: While retyping my comments on the following verses and the accompanying letter, I have inserted Mr. Darling's pencilled comments on the copy as he returned it to me.)

March 12, 19___

REHEARSAL. Changed a bit but seems to hang together better. Equipped is a prosy word but nearer the precise meaning than "allowed"?

AFTER STORM. Last stanza chosen and please let me keep the "why" instead of "doubt." Doubt is more passive — why is active — it can be a scorcher! Howsomever, if publication hangs on "why" being "doubt," change it. I do not feel it is all-important.

KADDISH. See my extended notes with the fair copy. (E.D. writes: I think it stands by itself now. But you could substitute that new sestet just as well if you like it better. Your choice!)

ALONE. Retired, with some sorrow, to the Hold file.
UP FROM THE GRAVE. Retired, with great relief.

AFTERGLOW: Now hear this! I am *not* underestimating, as you suggested, the strength of these bruises. I am being heavily ironic—they aren't "fatal," (you louse, you worm, you hurter of me)—and I'll survive but you have wounded me deeply, nonetheless, and you'd better be sorry! "Don't worry about it" really means "You'd damn well better worry about it." *You* don't "hear" them that way, so they may not succeed for a reader but they've never failed for a listener. This I want as is or not at all. (E.D. writes: The first point is good enough to carry it; I'd rather have *as is* than not at all.)

Afterglow (1948)

Like bruises—
> *red-streaked,*
> *dark-blue*
contusions—
linger your words
on the flesh of my being.
The colors are fading
> *but impressions remain*
red-angry, blue-mean—
still sore to the touch . . .
(Oh, don't worry about it—
> *bruises aren't fatal!)*

My goodness, I'm brave today. "Impressions" may very well be a weak word but I can't seem to come up with a better one. "But the prints still remain???" Nope. "Indentations" loses rhythm. I've been poking at myself all afternoon trying to find another word (could this be called the Method School of Writing?) but have only succeeded in making my arm sore.

Where do we stand now, Br'er Fox?

Do you realize I am in the process of getting educated? Right now I'm so excited by Eliot's essays on poets and poetry, it's hard to keep from collaring the nearest human and reading large gulps of it out loud.

So, proceeding on the unorthodox assumption that you — although an Editor — are human, (*E.D. writes: Very dangerous assumption*) Listen!

". . . In a poem which is neither didactic nor narrative, and not animated by any other social purpose, the poet may be concerned solely with expressing in verse this obscure impulse (inert embryo, creative germ). He does not know what he has to say until he has said it, and in the effort to say it he is not concerned with making other people understand anything. He is not concerned at this stage with other people at all: only with finding the right words, or anyhow, the least wrong words.

(Note: Underlining is mine; I also wrote "a TITLE?" and E.D. answered, "YES.")

"He is not concerned whether anybody else will ever listen to them or understand them. He is oppressed by a burden which he must bring to birth in order to obtain relief.

"Or, to change the figure of speech, he is haunted by a demon, a demon against which he feels powerless, because in its first manifestation it has no face, no name, nothing; and the words, the poem he makes, are a kind of form of exorcism of this demon.

". . . he is going to all that trouble, not in order to communicate with anyone, but to gain relief from acute discomfort; and when the words are finally arranged in the best arrangement he can find, he may experience a moment of exhaustion, appeasement, of absolution and of something very near annihilation, which is in itself indescribable. And then he can say to the poem 'Go away! Find a place for yourself in a book — and don't expect me to take any further interest in you.'

"The first effort of the poet should be to achieve clarity for himself, to assure himself that the poem is the right outcome of the process that has taken place. The most bungling form of obscurity is that of the poet who has not been able to express himself *to* himself; the shoddiest form is found when the poet is trying to persuade himself that he has something to say when he hasn't."

So perhaps he overdoes that "go away, poem" bit — but he describes the process beautifully. And if I fall into the "shoddiest" category, as I very well may, at least I have had some of the agony and some of the rapture associated with the making of a poem.

And I say again "thank you" for helping me believe in myself. *(E.D. has here underlined the three last words and written: "You must or perish.")* Sometimes, like now, I even find myself perched on the precarious edge of joy "somewhere I have never traveled gladly beyond" but more universally!

Crazily,
Carol

March 15, 19___

Dear Carol:

Let's leave it like this.

When you have done all the finishing you feel like doing, and when you have placed in my hands everything you hope to include in this volume, then give a loud signal and light the bonfires on the hilltops and go into hiding until you get my signal.

I, on the other hand, will put forth no finger to your file until the completion is perfect. Then, in one last burst, I'll make the final summary and get back to you with a proposition.

Okay?

Incidentally, I don't remember that quatrain about a pill, but it's terrific—my word, you may find, like the South American girl, that you're an octopus. *(Note: This was something I had scrawled off as a P.S.)*

Chemotherapy

Sometime, upon rising,
I won't take that pill —
(and see if I am
who I used to be still!)

Did you, honestly, think you had cancer? Jesuschrist,
I dunno whether I could handle *that* one. Are you okay?
Carol?

I don't give a damn what your psychoanalytic sibling
thinks. I know that for the painter, painting is therapeu-
tic — and maddening — but therapeutic. And I know that
for the writer, writing is therapeutic — and crucifying — but
therapeutic. And sometimes for the painter it is all sheer
joy; and sometimes for the writer it is an enormous day of
victory and the language wags its tail like a tamed wolf.

What's life without contrast? Without sour there *is* no
sweet.

Pax tibiscum,
Ed

March 19, 19__

Dear Mr. Darling:

Re: returned revisions of March 17 —

REHEARSAL. O.K., so start it with your uppercase
letter. In many cases I have to admit my choice of upper or
lower has been pure whimsy so any changing you wish to
do (with the possible exception of "inside the squirrel cage

at 3 A.M.") is fine by me. (And that "by me" is an intentional vulgarism. I do not wish to have you think I am ever *un*intentionally vulgar.)

AFTERGLOW. For the sake of that long-ago starry-eyed 18-year-old, fair copy you have stands.

KADDISH. A fair copy enclosed with new sestet. Please compare with the last one submitted, because I think it was tightened up a little and I did not keep a copy. Maledictions, sackcloth, ashes. If there are differences, return.

ONE OF THE PHASES. Returned with footnotes. Throw out if still unsuccessful by you.

That should be all—but on coming across a batch of possible revisions you returned some time ago (which I hid away because that was a Discouraged Day)—I found a couple which maybe didn't need too much work, so have made tentative fair copies. If they don't seem ready yet, throw them away, and I'll keep my copies in the Hold file for future use.

Sooooo—with the possible exception of KADDISH, this is all.

That bonfire isn't so easy to light—all of a sudden I feel like questioning every single damn line of every single damn verse and even with two tranquillizers placating the viscera, am shaky as hell about it.

Your last letter helped shore me up tremendously and I *am* "okay." Now and forever amen.

We heard Auden read at Colby College Friday night. I know you are busy but have to tell you a little about it (and will send you my two column review in the Maine Sunday Telegram when it gets printed). He looked older than 60, lines like Icelandic runes engraved in his face; very dignified but with that marvelous understated humor and sense of word-fun. His poetry has kept me going sometimes when all other "philosophies" failed and the most blessed thing about what he read at Colby is that there was not a drop—not one fractional quintessential drop of self-pity which surrounds so many of the so-called "moderns" (company included) like a hallucinatory morass. It is today as if "joy" had become a dirty word, taboo, unspeakable. He cares but he doesn't get all bogged down in it. "With the farming of a verse/ make a vineyard of the curse/ sing of human unsuccess/ in a rapture of distress/ in the deserts of the heart/ let the healing fountain start/ in the prison of his days/ teach the free man how to praise" and from another poem: "Love gives no excuse to evil done for love . . ." etc.

I believe that,
Carol

Today's the first of April
and I am April's fool—
a muddy-footed jester . . .

Good afternoon!

Here is, until you have some second or third thoughts, my last blast. It is a rewrite of REUNION—tighter and more effective than the first. There have been sad syntactical problems with this—one of the first times around I had the "monster stones" climbing like "air-exuberant birds"! Reminds me of the sixth grade spelling-dictation sentence which breaks me up each time I read it solemnly from the workbook: "Mother made a delicious salad."

I think getting a booklet of verse into a final form must involve some sort of PhD thesis block. All of a sudden I question each one of the damn things and could start rewriting from start to finish and then over again and probably die with it not finished.

These are not good days. The teaching is so difficult I am overcome by enormous fatigue which my husband characterizes as neurotic and I am fearful he may be right. Usually there is a regenerative process in the classroom, a kind of joyous feedback, but I've not been able to establish that this year and can feel myself turning into a monster. If I am offered a high school English job at Yarmouth I shall take it. This will be scarifying but it will force me into new reading and learning and close attention to many authors, all of which should have worthy impact on my writing.

If I have already told you this, I'm sorry—and don't mention anything about it in your letters, please. My husband and I have gone along tandem for a good many years and there have been other periods when resentment has built up because one partner (usually me — but not always) is doing more coasting than pedaling.

And you are not a marriage counselor, forsooth — I 'umbly begs your pardon. What I should do, since I am all alone here at the lodge, is to go outside and yell at the top of my lungs, over and over until I am sick of hearing it and the loons begin to laugh — *it is not easy to be a wife mother teacher and a goddamned poet. It is not easy. . . .*

Etc.

Carol

P.S. An overamplification of the present condition follows:

Autobiographical Sketch #1223

Lump too large to swallow —
*   pressure on the chest —*
and fantasies
*   force her to the antiseptic den,*
where, walled around
*   by evident afflictions*
of old age,
*   she reads a lurid magazine.*
The pages shake. Finally,
*   the M.D. writes*
perfunctory prescriptions —
*   "to soothe anxiety*
and ease the pain."

Almost better
* cells gone wild*
than having to admit
* conscience sovereign*
to flesh. Unchristian
* scientist, she has to face*
what caused the heavy mass —
* or else submit*
to biochemistry's mock cure.
* Healing by a numbing*
of the spirit is not recovery.
* "Turn off the mind, O Librium,*
and liberate the flesh."
* "What happens to the soul?"*
one asks — but even
* dapper druggists*
have no answer.

It still may hurt to live
* while tranquillized,*
but one can giggle mindlessly
* about the pain —*
and guilt is gilded
* with a rosy glow.*
(Does she still remind herself
*   of someone whom*
*   she used to know?)*

Bleeagh,
C.

April 6, 19___

Dear Carol:

This acknowledges receipt of two more poems, AUTO-
BIOGRAPHICAL SKETCH and REUNION. I think I like them
both. So I'll just add them to what I've already put aside
until I've finished other stuff I have of yours. This is going
to be very tight living here until after General Assembly in
Denver, end of the month — so have patience!

Best,
Ed

May 7, 19___

A Letter To An Editor

Dear Sir:

It really isn't so long since I heard from you, I guess;
maybe it seems longer to me than it does to . . .

Hi!

I certainly hope you are feeling all right (physically, as
well as mentally, I mean) and nothing has happened to
make you change your . . .

Dear E.D.

Just the other day I was thinking about you and could
almost picture you at your desk with all those really impor-
tant things to get accom . . .

Well hello!

How's the weather been down in your bailiwick? Here in my bailiwick it's mostly been fog, and after a while it really begins to get depress . . .

Gentleman:

People aren't real, are they? One just sort of invents them to suit one's need of the moment as one goes along: that's not original but it's interesting, don't you . . .

Director of Publications, etc:

After all, if a snail is stupid enough to come out of its shell, it's too damn dumb to bother to step around for very long, right? Snails belong *inside* their . . .

Dear Mr. Darling:

Are you chuckling at all?

CBH

Dear Carol:

It's pretty unforgivable, I'll admit; I've been awfully slow. And to sit here and tell you why would only compound the injury . . .

Herewith, back to you: REUNION B; I'm choosing A. Plus ONE OF THE PHASES, which means a lot to you but not to me; I think you're overworking that old moon. You're probably terribly introspective anyhow — *c'est moi qui parle,* for God's sake. Plus TEMPI with a question. I'm keeping FIRST STEPS, IN MEMORIAM, KADDISH, REUNION A.

Are you ready? Do you want to have one more look at my copy of the total book? Any last thoughts? Want an introduction? Because if you don't want to do any of these things, then I plan to go to the printer. If you do, here's your chance.

It is to laugh, actually. For three or four weeks I am sitting on my attractive bottom doing nothing about Carol Hudson; and the next minute I am up and shouting, hurry, hurry, hurry.

Well, don't hurry. First, think it over; then either release the manuscript or ask to see the final work once more, and I'll act accordingly.

Blessings,
Ed

. . . your "small disheveled muse"
(for Elizabeth Coatsworth Beston)

Nor will I question
this sudden sunshine
in my blood —
natural or artifice,
it is the precious dictator
returned.

Here is discovery
of ancient health; the childish talent
for rapt and joyful inquiry
into presents;

here too, the woman's need
for shaping words, keeping life.
I will accept your gift —
use it tenderly.

First Steps (1958)

Smiling,
> *the tiny great-grandmother*
bends to the baby
> *and holds out her wrinkle-soft hands;*
Bubbling with laughter,
> *Anne easily crosses*
> *four generations*
on a clearly-marked, well-traveled
welcoming pathway called love.
(Sweet stumbler —
> *might there always be*
a loving hand stretched out to thee!)

June 3, 19___

Dear Mr. Darling:

I *knew* as soon as I sent that silly note I would hear from you. Sorry. Would you be surprised to learn that ever since your letter arrived this morning, CBH has been mouth-dry, knee-knock scared? What some other Me had all this audacity? All derring-do is suddenly derring-don't. Instant Panic sets in . . .

But yes, I do release the manuscript with the following questions and amendments:

1) Please omit FIRST NIGHT ALONE (he retained it) and SLOW LEARNER (he retained it). The ending of FIRST NIGHT is poor and SLOW L. is too ditty. This leaves 45 verses according to my enclosed list.

2) Is it too corny to have several "dedications" on poems which were written for specific people? Hopefully not — although I defer to your judgment. (Note: "Dedicate until the return of the cows," he pencilled in response.)

3) Shouldn't credit be given to the *NYS Education Journal* for THE ROOM and SELF-CONFIDENCE; *Free Lance* for FLUFF and *Portland Sunday Telegram* for REUNION. I just got paid $5.00 for the last-mentioned — my first payment for verse!

4) Have we a title? If EVE still reads satisfactorily to you, let's use it for title and first poem.

5) What about the order? They are in an awful muddle right now. I would be happy to have you unscramble them but will attempt it if you so desire. I think there are better things than EVE, but I'm no judge. *(Note: "We could, if you insist," E.D. wrote. "This is still open. I don't think it expresses the idea of this book as well as what we have.")*

Brad Greeley came out the other evening to help choose some verses for me to read as part of his worship service tomorrow. He thinks you are "just great." Me too.

Lily-livered Carol

First Night Alone at the Lake

All day I pushed the shadows back
*   even though my senses knew*
the sun would set, the lake turn black,
*   I battle dark the long night through.*
Behind the cabin, forest tall
*   would crouch more closely than by day,*
while things beyond the windowed wall
*   moved in their stealthy, unnamed way.*
Tensions rise in tightened throat,
*   trembles in this coward skin,*
near flickering lamp the pale moths float,
*   and pulse create a dreadful din.*
This black-bleak elemental awe
*   singly I'd have to face*
till, morning won, the rising sun
*   returned me sanity and space.*
Each lovely day is worth the fright
*   I think —* whenever it is light;
At dusk I, shaking, know I'm mad
*   to stay alone, both scared and sad.*
But though I cannot conquer fear
*   at least I meet it every year!*

Slow Learner

"She can't understand
    the value of money,"
our daughter's report card said;
implying (though very politely),
    she wasn't quite right in the head.

But teacher, I thought,
    in horror and shock, —
how can this possibly be?

Like every suburban family
we assess people's worth financially,
we talk about money every day,
her share for chores is reckoned pay —
complaining of taxes, bills, and status
we show her nothing happens gratis . . .

So she may be a darling,
    she may be a honey —
but 'she can't understand the value of money!'

Oh well, it may not be too late;
    after all, she's only eight.

June 5, 19___

Dear Carol:

One thing you have learned in your dealings with other people this year — and that's how to be impatient without showing it very much. I must say you are now an adept; and you may regard this sheet as your diploma . . .

Great minds, they do tell, inhabit similar if not the same channels; and this must be so, because your very cute card of May 24 just arrived, and mine to you must this day be in your hands. If it's not osmosis, then it's mental telepathy!

Live forever,
Ed

June 7, 19__

Dear Carol:

So now all of a sudden I'm "Mr. Darling." Jesus H. Christ! Stop being in awe of the printed word . . . A vast amount of material is printed every year which cannot compare in any way with what you've turned out. That's the truth.

I'm returning herewith a copy of FOREBODING, explained in my note.

Also herewith is your letter to me, marked with my pencil.

If you have credits to give, you should let me have a little paragraph saying, "Four of these poems have appeared elsewhere. I should like to express appreciation to (etc.) All the others appear in this volume for the first time."

That paragraph should be on a separate piece of paper from your introduction.

I have entirely revamped your order in the wan attempt to make a pattern which can be seen and appreciated. Maybe it doesn't jell. See what you think.

Now then — when I have your answer to all *this,* I guess we can go to press. Hokay? Lightly, baby, take it easy! It's only ink and paper . . .

Cordially,
Ed

(Note: On June 10, helped by a Portland poet-friend in a last-ditch, all-night and truly heroic effort, I was able to send Mr. Darling an order of verses and suggested section titles, along with the following note: "Please don't shoot me if I say I don't even remember an Autobiographical Sketch — perhaps something I scrawled off for you? Include it anywhere you think fit — and I hope you approve of this ordering.")

June 14, 19__
Post school,
Pre supper,
One dexamyl up

FINAL FINAL FINAL FINAL

1) Here is SELF CONFIDENCE — your copy probably blew away at the Cape or was stolen by a sea gull.

2) Omit AUTOBIOGRAPHICAL SKETCH — I had later called it PRESCRIPTION FOR HYPOCHONDRIA and under neither title can it be considered finished. I was just trying to get some sympathy.

3) Sara is Teasdale. Sometimes we are sisters-under-the-obvious & thin-skin.

4) You did not say whether or not the order of service was accepted but suspect you would have told me if it were not.

5) Maybe I just have post-natal depression but my bones ache ferociously with end-of-school fatigue. And I am *such* a sweet teacher—

"Armand, if you open your mouth once more, I am going to *strangle* you!"

"Does this class want to stay an extra *day?*"

"But Mr. Lerch, sir, I didn't *mean* to be 37 and a half sessions off in my attendance book!"

"No, Mrs. Nunes, I do *not* remember where I put Tommy's giant tarantula made out of expensive plastic which he left on my chair last November . . ."
ad nauseum.

Plus, older son goes to Germany next week, we move into our new house in less than 10 days, German boy (son's exchange) arrives June 28, then we have to go back to N.Y.S. to settle *that* house and go on from there to Smoke Lake—if I am still breathing.

A simple little black border around the title will be all that is necessary . . .

Mournfully,
Carol

P.S. I apologize for being so Eeyorish. It's simple exhaustion—and not writing.

(Note: Scribbled on the preceding pages, along with sundry "O.K.s" were these typical E.D. comments: "Go out somewhere and raise hell, Teach"; "Teasdale! I know half her stuff by heart." And circled in a black magic marker at the page bottom were the still holy, wholly unbelievable words: "Going now to the printer . . . E.D.")

August 15, 19___

Dear Armie:

     . . . Early in July I urged you to let me have word on the poetry of Carol Hudson and you responded that your typesetter was on vacation and would soon return.

    Now again I have a query from Mrs. Hudson. What can I tell her *this* time? My last correspondence on this subject asked you for an estimate and gave the limits within which I could publish. I really cannot leave this *in vacuuo;* I must start moving . . .

So, what's the word?
Edward Darling

Copy to Carol Hudson

August 17, 19___

Dear Mrs. Hudson:

The printer phoned Mr. Darling today, and he has promised that we will have proofs for *Destination Unknown* before Labor Day. Therefore, as Mr. Darling would say,

> Be of good cheer!
> Viriginia Allen
> Secretary

September 5, 19___

Dear Carol:

Here's your set of proofs.

Please check carefully and let me have the sheets back as soon as it's convenient.

This ought to make you feel a little better! Hm?

> Best,
> Ed

September 10, 19___
Too Late on a
Tired Sunday night

My typewriter feels tongue-tied — it has seemed a long time not to be in touch with whoever E.D. is and so much has gone on in between it is hard to know where not to start.

I have proof-read as carefully (twice-over) as I can, and return the proofs herewith. The only thing missing is the dedication page — something about an Uncertain Vine which sounds pretty damned Cute, but right now *all* of the words look in need of adjective overhauling and massive doses of Vitamin B1. The only recommendation for their existence I can cling to after the keelhauling I had at Bread Loaf is that they are not phony. No, that's fake morbidity — they do speak to *people* even if they don't speak to *poets* and expecially to John Frederick Nims whom I hate with a purple passion. Julia Stair knows why.

Bread Loaf was a two week, 20 hour-a-day Happening. It was An Experience. It was Limbo. It never really existed. I lost track of CBH the first day and woke up 14 days later back in South Freeport. My brain was like a ping-pong ball with Norman Mailer playing Archibald MacLeish. Some day I hope to be able to put it in words.

If You and *Destination Unknown* hadn't been anchors to windward, I might really been blown off course. Or sunk.

One earnestly vibrating-type of female at B.L. said she too was really a poet but her verses were the children of her heart and she could never share them with the crass multitude.

Well, she's probably on the right track for the sake of the multitude, but as I look back over the past year and a half, I'll be damned if I'll recant on all the work on my part and on your part which has gone into this book.

Yet, dear Mr. Darling, I think the anesthetic has worn off and the pangs are frightening me. There are many, many things I wish I had done differently — and better.

Hell's bells, I'm beginning to sound like Sydney Carton.

> Yours, with great confidence — in *you!*
> Carol

(Note: The preceding letter was sent along with a new verse that used the word "hesychastic"; I noted that it was too show-offey, probably.)

September 14, 19___

Dear Carol:

Yes, I *told* Gobin *(Note: Gobin Stair, then the Director of Beacon Press, was one of the experts on tap at Bread Loaf)* to look you up; but the silent bastard will not say anything except that he found you interesting and felt that you found *me* interesting; he said he wasn't going to place himself in any middle position and get his ears slapped back. A great man, old Gobe, really great; he carries a terrible burden of responsibility and does it — mostly — with sweetness and charm. And he saved my *Old Quotes* from being merely pedestrian with his wild and unbuckled art work.

I disagree with you that "hesychastic" is show-off; it's a perfectly good English word with a most specific and pointed meaning — beatific vision; and in a way it is cognate with *omphalopsychite:* one who stares at his navel. This is *delight,* not show-off.

Let me also give you *envoûtement,* in case you don't have it: this is sticking pins in a doll to curse someone you hate; casting a spell. You sound as if you could use such a term after Bread Loaf.

I like SPRING MOMENT but I agree with you — let's not fool around now. Let's get the book in the works. GROWL is rather terrific . . . Well, let's start collecting them just in case, hm?

1 - Dedication page. The manuscript the printer returned to me begins on page 3, so I assume he has the first two pages, title and dedication, at the plant. I have not seen those two pages in print.

2 - In Part I, THE COUNTRY WITHIN, you are quite right; the printer has placed the verses in exact reverse, the last being first and the first last. *Do you care?* If so, I will instruct him to fix that. The other Parts seem to be correct. But if it doesn't matter, let's not trouble the printer. *This is your decision.*

3 - You seem to be troubled about the order in Part V. It appears according to our paging — the printer made no error. Since the pages are numbered, we must bear the cost of rearranging and renumbering. If this is what you want, then send me the order you finally choose. This is rather too bad: the printer did follow script.

4 - Your corrections on AFTERGLOW are clear. We can *get* space between the 1 and the !

5 - AGAINST COMMUNICATION. Sorry, you're wrong. No lines are left out. Printer has followed script exactly. Don't forget you've revised some of these babies . . .

6 - THE ROOM, page 23. I disagree that "is" must be inserted. The meaning is utterly clear: you picture a world filled with music and cheerful chatter. Then you have a semicolon. That I'd change to a colon, but I wouldn't add "is" at all. No need for it.

7 - TRIAL BY WATER, page 30. Why do you want to cut "not to be leapt into unaware, —lacking care." Your other corrections here are printer's errors and will be corrected. Do you insist on cutting these two lines?

8 - P. 32—printer's error; you're right; a line is missing.

9 - P. 51—REUNION: Of course the whole point in our give-and-take previously was to make sure that this sort of thing would not happen; and we finally went to the printer with our order to set type. However, if you've changed again, I'll have this one reset according to your wishes. It is amateur work, this: revising when the proofs come in, I mean. We should not have gone to the printer unless we had agreed on what we wanted—and I thought we had. However, I have to admit that you're not the first author to see what he wanted after it had been set. But it's very bad to do—However, I have marked the thing for resetting.

Well, there we are—all 57 pages.

You realize that you have to answer some questions raised in this letter. I will hold onto ms. and proofs until I hear from you; at which point I will send both to the compositor.

Be of good cheer; you found a number of important printer's errors, and on the whole you were very good about letting things alone. I had to scold at P. 51 to justify my existence, I guess.

Cordially,
Ed

September 20, 10__

Dear Carol:

It suddenly occurs to me that you asked to have a copy of *Old Quotes*.

I could swear I'd sent you one long ago, but perhaps not. Anyway, a copy is on its way now, and I expect a little *appreciation,* y'hear? By which I mean you're not to judge the book from the first three pages, but only from the first ten. After that, if you give up and throw up your hands and God knows what else, I will find no fault.

Incidentally, there will be no "bill," for God's sake. GOD indeed . . .

Best,
Ed

Note: I do not have a copy of my letter to which his next one responds — evidently it had to do with my first baffled attempts at "teaching" high school students; it was a question, all that first year, of whether they or I had charge of the classroom . . .)

Sept. 22, 19__

Dear Carol:

I can't help envying you as you start teaching just-short-of-illiterate 11th graders. My first teaching job was in

Salem, New Hampshire, where they had a race-track where at least one driver was killed in almost every race; and you can imagine how that Summer Attraction affected the kids in the "largest Armenian colony in New England." Are your kids Beats, Hippies? You're lucky you ain't got *city* kids, even so. You ought to try them out on BOOTS (Kipling) or THE CONGO (Lindsay) if you want to see 'em whoop and holler . . . Fantastic rhythm.

Well, gal, I guess we're set. You've been very patient; and yet you've made your independent stand for what you really wanted. I like to *believe* I have not overwhelmed you or forced you at any critical point. I meant *not* to.

Personally, I wouldn't *dare* see the doctor. That I'm still here is miracle enough for me. I know that's an ignorant reaction; but it's strongly motivated by various fears which we will lump into the misnomer, distaste. I have no taste for doctors' offices.

You're really wonderful. Having nothing to worry about, this woman worries about having nothing to worry about. But have faith: she'll *find* something!

Right now all she has to have is patience. . . .

Blessings,
Ed

P.S. Vocabulary word: *Vitiate.* Student sentence: Because it was left too long in the sun, the milk vitiated. That's one I've never forgotten.

October 2, 19___

Dear Carol:

Ten thousand thanks for the review (*of his and Ashley Montagu's book, The Prevalence of Nonsense*) from the *Evening Express.* I wish the large papers would be half so generous!

Naturally I'm delighted that you like *Old Quotes.* Most people apparently just don't get the point. A weekly on Cape Cod accused the author of suggesting to people that they should lie to get ahead . . . Heigh-ho.

Social historian. Mm-yaas. And why not? They had to say *something:* they couldn't say "anthropologist Ashley Montagu and biped Edward Darling." Although I think that would have been more descriptive, at that.

Anyhow, blessings and my thanks.

Cordially,
Ed

November 14, 19___

Dear Carol:

Any day now I expect to see finished copies of your book, and therefore I must prepare some promotion to try to get the work known and sold. We won't be able to put much money into that part of it, but let's do the best we can in the circles we can reach!

First of all, the author will receive 20 copies free. What you do with these so-called "vanity" copies is none of my business. After that, if you need more copies, they are yours at the standard author's discount of 40% off list price.

"Promotion copies" differ from vanity copies in that they are sent free to reviewers and persons who might help get the book talked about. Have you got anybody in mind who might write the review for our denominational journal? Maybe Don Johnston? Let me know of any other people you think might help and to whom I should send copies.

In addition, I need further identification of you, in order to make the author an interesting person whom one might be interested in hearing. Are you a Unitarian? Of what church do you consider yourself a member? How long have you been interested in writing? Why poetry? Do you find it therapeutic or disturbing? What ambitions do you have? When were you married and how many children are there, and anything else that's personal and to the point. I'm asking for what the lads call a Curriculum Vitae, you see. To be modest or withdrawn at this point is out of the question, so don't do it. *I'll* do any editing that's necessary.

> And hurry up---!
> Ed

> November 20, 19___

Mr. Darling:

The following is a result of inviting my "top-level" English class to write my biography for you. Only one girl dared hand her effort in (although there was a lot of satisfied giggling going on all period); I feel she was completely successful . . .

Dear Sirs:

In response to your request that I tell you about myself, I am writing this letter.

I have had a rare disease since childhood which led me to take up writing. After all, lockjaw is hardly conducive to public speaking.

At the age of seven, I married. She is a wonderful woman and has made me very happy. At present we have 12 children and expect four more with the next week.

I live in a fine old house on an island in a sewer. We have a slight transportation problem, of course, but then . . .

> Yours in Christ,
> Carol Hudson
> (Sue Flint)

I'll do it, I'll do it.

My mother-in-law has been staying with us since her husband died and this sort of fills in the hours.

Lewisohn says all of my writing is typical WASP-three-name-lady-poet. If I protest, he calls me anti-semitic.

I would love to have Don review *Destination Unknown*. I'll send some other suggestions for promotional targets when I put the autobiographical material on paper. It will just serve to *discourage* people, though — and I am not being shy or withdrawn, thank you — it's just damned dull.

> Carol

November 27, 19___

Dear Carol:

You are a jewel, and no mistake. Like most really *valuable* jewels, you can scratch sharply enough to make a mark on glass if necessary; but there is a genuine vital excitement in you which breathes of life and derring-do and so forth, and I like it; I like it.

1) Thanks for the information. I got what I asked for in every respect.

2) The MacLeish letter: please write and tell him that your editor is badgering you with a request for permission to quote, "Carol Hudson is no slight singer." I'm *telling* you, baby, those words will sell this thing, and no fooling . . . Get me the permission! And don't stand there all day — get moving!

3) If you can inspire work like that from a junior, you're a real teacher and the kid is lucky to have you. Her final paragraph is very very funny, and the rest is better than average "humerous" writing.

More later,
Ed

(Note: Since Archibald MacLeish's comment was really no more than a polite response to a verse I had written about his reading at Bread Loaf, I didn't want to ask him for permission to quote it for an advertising blurb. However, pushed by Mr. Darling, I did — and should have abided by my first instincts. He gave permission but it was easy to see that he felt "used." The next communication from E.D. was a handwritten scrawl occupying a full sheet of paper — and the excitement of seeing the book for the first time drove all other thoughts from my mind . . .)

CAROL!
Merry Christmas and
heartiest congratulations!
It's *beautiful*. You are
forbidden to see anything
but beauty here—hear?

Hear, hear!
ED

Your bulk shipment is on its way—

(Note: Mr. Darling's next letter is in response to my complaint that the Portland bookstores had ordered copies of Destination Unknown *only to receive cards saying "No longer available." This, I told him bitterly, must be what a psychologist might call a self-fulfilling title.)*

December 14, 19__

Dear Carol:

How wonderful to see that everything is normal—customers ordering books which are "no longer available," especially when they are entirely new and in good supply. Ah yes; this is my life.

Well, I think *that's* straightened out. If you had *only* told me who they are, what the addresses are, and what quantity they wanted, I could today ship the books. But poets aren't supposed to be able to consider such mundane matters—they just beef and let it go at that.

If anybody else complains, tell 'em to write direct to me.

I've done a special ad for the *Register-Leader* which should appear in January. Too late for Christmas, but this is a book for all seasons.

Your poem FRAGMENTS has been set in special white letters on one of those bulletin boards in the elevator at 25 Beacon, so everybody in the building has seen at least one poem and knows the author's name. A special plug has gone out in the Ministers' Packet. I gave a free copy to every one of the District Executives and told them to talk it up.

Let me know of any comment you receive!

Merry Christmas,
Ed

Fragment

Although a tarnished soul
        can never shine like new again,
with adequate abrasive
        and rough scrubbing,
hopefully
it may acquire
        a dignified patina —
before being
discarded.

December 15, 19___

Dear Beefy Editor:

Gawd'elpus, I'm sorry to have sounded whiney. Ain't never had nuthin' published befer now, see? It's all sorta new and strange . . .

I have sent a card to the bookstores asking them to try again.

Am I also being difficult if I ask whether your office has had a chance to send out the "review copies" to the list of people I sent you? Some have asked me when I thought they might get these copies because they wanted to do it before Xmas if possible.

Yes, I suppose that's being difficult. If ever I am a Real Nuisance, ignore me. It's good for my paranoia.

I am really terribly pleased with and proud of the booklet—but a little afraid to admit it for fear of being smacked down by the gods—again.

Later

Enclosed is the first review. Eleanor is a good writer (she even has her own *agent!*) although her approach here is a bit too folksy—(surely I never "yearned" in quite that way?) at least it takes up a lot of space and when you're being paid by the column inch, that's important.

Lovely letter from Don J. about it, too.

After New Year's holiday hangovers I want to suggest

a list of ex-Bread Loafers who are teacher-poets to send books to — maybe even ol' Cadillac Ciardi!

Pot-valiantly,*
Carol

*in the Elizabethan sense of the word

December 18, 19__

Dear Carol:

From now on the best and quickest and most efficient way to get copies of your book out into the stores and churches will be to . . . let it go through the regular order department. Remember you have to expect to wait three weeks at this time of year . . .

Hell's redhot bells, I guess we've been slow on those review copies; but they'll go out now. Egad, I'm glad you reminded me. I've been out of the office too much in the last three weeks. Sorry!

You are not a real nuisance. You are a real author. There is a subtle — but distinguishable — difference.

Let me have *all the beefs* every time. That's the only way we'll get this straightened out. Bit by bit your work will get known, and then it will sell — because it's good. It's really good. I say so.

Best,
Ed

(Note: About this time I received a copy of the highly fictional advertising blurb E.D. had sent out in the ministers' packets. Parts of it are quoted below.)

"Now your correspondent would like to make a personal statement. Carol Hudson is skillful, poignant, earthy, sensitive, troubled, uncertain, urgent, appreciative, fearful and at times humorous when she laughs at herself. These are poems about nature, humanity, love, children, beauty, disgust, purpose, meaning, indignation — probings for meaning. Above all they are human. I feel so sure about this book that I'll guarantee it: customers can return unsold copies for credit if I'm wrong. She's a real poet. Here is a charming, inexpensive Christmas gift . . .

Do try this one on your book table!

Edward Darling"

11 P.M. fireside time
December 28, 19__

Dear Receiver of Unwanted Confidences:

I'm feeling like Lady M. again and this time you are immediately responsible so I'll not even apolgize for writing. I tried to sleep but kept chewing away at the bars, so got up, rebuilt the fire, reheated the coffee, retrieved a pen from the writing table and returned to discussing my magnificent problem with you.

First, thank you for sending the January *Register-Leader,* the packet letter and the copies of your letters to Jones Book Shop and A. MacLeish. I had not yet sent him a copy of the book and am glad you did. (Just hope it doesn't make him wince and feel all-over retractious!) Your letter was just right, and by that I mean it sounded as it would have if I had written it myself. What majestic word-manipulators we are, we are!

So what is my current complaint? Simply, I am aghast at seeing the adjectives (in the ad and the packet) you used in conjunction with my name. That is some other Carol — not the one I know and certainly not the one my family endures. This She spoken of in the ad is a truly remarkable person — I'd like to meet her sometime.

Now don't get perturbed, yet — hear me think this quandary through. Would it sell any less books to come a little closer to truth?

I am a coward, crying my fears out loud in an attempt to find comfort; I am a liar trying to learn to accept the truthfulness of my deceit; I am a plotter seeking something worth plotting; I am my own enemy, trying to make peace with myself?

I am *not* a girl — I merely got stuck in my development toward emotional maturity at about age 19. These things you have said about me are only my illusions — my projections into never-never land.

The only real respect I have for myself is that I am maintaining one family's status-quo at some cost to my own ego-needs — and if that sounds like the worst type of psyche-seepage, *you're right!*

Who was it warned me I'd have to be willing to go down into the marketplace and scrap — oh yes, — Edward Darling. Well, I have. I've been pushing DU until I feel like a fifth rate fullerbrush man. And I'll continue to do so, but I didn't have any idea that seeing undeserved compliments in print would hit me like brickbats. (Brickbats, I expected . . .)

Oh wow.

"Well," he says, crunching this sorry letter and tossing it toward the wastebasket—"what the hell does she expect me to say?"

Ah dunno, Br'er Darling, ah dunno. But I had to get it out of my stuffy bosom before I could get to sleep. Anyway, *you* stay undeluded and don't ever begin to believe your own advertising copy, okay?

Miserably,
Carol

P.S. My sons now refer to me as their old earthy mother . . .

P.S.#2 Bless you—my inability to accept what the blurbs say is not *your* problem. I should just smile sweetly and bask in the warmth of the words. Maybe I will have to practice the Art of Accepting Artificial Accolades from Aditors? I feel much better. Thanks for listening!

January 17, 19__

Dear Carol:

They tell me at our headquarters that *Destination Unknown* is selling very well—that is, to the wanderers who come into the building. I learn from the Beacon Order Department that most of the orders received are for multiple copies—that is, five or ten and sometimes more. Most of this is the result of the Packet notice. We won't begin to feel the January ad results for another couple of weeks.

The minister at Fort Lauderdale has just asked for a review copy, adding, "if it's what you say it is, we should be ordering copies for our members." Well, despite what the author thinks, it *is* what I said it was.

I'm wondering what would happen if I ran another ad and characterized the author as: a coward, crying her fears out loud in the darkness; a liar, trying to learn to accept the truthfulness of her deceit—and the rest of it? By God, I might try . . .

Don Johnston has written a lovely review. March issue.

Best,
Ed

April 8, 19__

Sir Edward the First:

The rest of my world is attending the funeral of a freshman who was killed last week by a baseball. I am perversely writing to people I like best and trying to forget his parents' grief and his girl's and the loss of his fine writer's brain. In our literary magazine he wrote; "The Ladybug was so big and frightening that people came from all around to run away from her."

After a long drought of no words, I am still old-pruney, though I've been reading enough of Emily again to feel a bit replenished.

Three items: 1) I've never seen the March reveiw
2) Is DU selling at all? At all how much?
3) How I miss "working" with you—

that marching-on-to-Jesus feeling. And I despise whomsoever is the object of your editorial attentions now. Grrrrr.

If any of this is cryptic, excuse me. A day and a night of Emily's letters has left me unsyntaxed.

Wildly,
Carol

P.S. I have two winter pomes I like some.

P.S.#2 If I were a Real Poet, we could publish some of our correspondence. How long can *you* live? I mean, if you would only kindly live for a long, long time, by the age of 80 — if there is still a world and if there are still people who read living in that world — I should be getting some kind of recognition — if only for longevity and determination. THEN they'd read our letters!

P.S.#3 Do you see why I will never want to confront you corporeally? I can't talk too good!

Note: Sometime that summer of let-down and withdrawal symptoms, I sent Edward Darling some new verses and semi-seriously accused him of abandoning his former authors.)

August 13, 19__

Dear Carol:

Without ever having seen you, I have loved you. Left you, I never have. That is a goddam canard, and I do not refer to an ocean liner. You are the most successful poet I have ever sponsored entirely on my own hunches. Successful in the sense that everybody who sees the book admits it's a honey. Nobody says it's a bundle of crap. And lots of people have tried to get me to take *their* sheafs of verse as Number Two in the series, but none has seriously competed with your verse, and that's a damned fact.

I'm holding the lovely ONLY THE SMELL OF THE VIOLETS for space in the magazine. It may be, and probably will be, ten years. But the poem is good; the words are well-chosen; the thought is crisp, tough, sinewy — mystical. The MUMMY poem is also good. Jesus, you have the variety — *that's* what it is about you. *Everything* tingles you . . .

Okay, now the feathers are back in place.

Lissen, there is no withdrawing from a friendship. And I have no wish to withdraw from ours. We may never do another book — or we may do a dozen. But the personality of Carol Hudson is so firmly imbedded in my mind that every other Carol I know gets called "Hudson" until I remember to sort out my people. So let's have no more backing and filling about this: you're an important author to me; I'm an important editor to you; and neither one of us ever got echoed in the vastness of the world's marketplaces and auditoriums. So, by all means, be it. Our personal relationship, meanwhile, is untouchable. Stet.

In short, if you do not feel free to turn to me at any time with any problem — simply because you want to — then everything has been wasted. So cut that out. I regard you as difficult but necessary. Same as you do me. How many people can you be as candid with and know that nothing has been disturbed?

Goodbye forever. I never expect to hear from you again, ever.

Not until next week, anyway.

Say, Monday?

Okay. It's a date!

Love,
Ed

Birches in Spring

Framed by my window,
    blurred by fog,
branches tangle together,
brushed against the smoky sky
like some medieval tapestry,
    outlines dimmed
by centuries of being.

    Green
is only a tiny suggestion
above the dark limbs;
    a leafy
reminder of change
more enduring than art.

Hidden in mist, a prophet
with healing in his throat
sings like a thrush.

This commonplace pattern

fog   bird   tree

forms my direction. Shrouded
in shadow, clearly
unable to see, I
shall continue to be
        blessed
by the ancient reminder
that songs can be spun
from instinctive belief
    in the green,
    in the sun.